THE HINDU-YOGI SCIENCE OF BREATH

The benefits of controlling mouth and nose breathing, as demonstrated in traditional yoga practice

William Walker Atkinson

GENERAL PRESS

Published by
GENERAL PRESS
4805/24, Fourth Floor, Krishna House
Ansari Road, Daryaganj, New Delhi - 110002
Ph : 011-23282971, 45795759
E-mail : generalpressindia@gmail.com

www.generalpress.in

First Edition : 2023

ISBN : 9789354995194

Published by Azeem Ahmad Khan for General Press

The Hindu-Yogi Science of Breath

BESTSELLING NON-FICTION

- Abraham Lincoln by Lord Charnwood, ISBN: 9789380914251
- Annihilation of Caste by Dr B.R. Ambedkar, ISBN: 9789390492732
- Be What You Wish by Neville Goddard, ISBN: 9789387669550
- Civilization and Its Discontents by Sigmund Freud, ISBN: 9789387669499
- Guerrilla Warfare by Ernesto Che Guevara, ISBN: 9789354990366
- How I Made 2 Millions in the Stock Market by N. Darvas, ISBN: 9789389716283
- Jail Diary and Other Writings by Bhagat Singh, ISBN: 9789390492398
- Man-eaters of Kumaon by Jim Corbett, ISBN: 9789354990731
- My Experiments with Truth by Mahatma Gandhi, ISBN: 9789387669291
- Relativity by Albert Einstein, ISBN: 9789380914220
- Reminiscences of a Stock Operator by Edwin Lefevre, ISBN: 9788194764816
- Scientific Healing Affirmations by P. Yogananda, ISBN: 9789389716344
- Student's Encyclopedia of G.K. by Azeem Ahmad Khan, ISBN: 9789380914190
- The Art of War by Sun Tzu, ISBN: 9789380914893
- The Book of Five Rings by Miyamoto Musashi, ISBN: 9789354991202
- The Diary of a Young Girl by Anne Frank, ISBN: 9789380914312
- The Game of Life and How to Play It by F. Scovel Shinn, ISBN: 9789387669390
- The Law of Success by Napoleon Hill, ISBN: 9788180320927
- The Origin of Species by Charles Darwin, ISBN: 9788180320453
- The Power of Your Subconscious Mind by Joseph Murphy, ISBN: 9788180320958
- The Psychopathology of Everyday Life by Sigmund Freud, ISBN: 9789388118071
- The Richest Man in Babylon by George S. Clason, ISBN: 9789387669369
- The World as I See It by Albert Einstein, ISBN: 9789388118125
- Why I am an Atheist and Other Works by Bhagat Singh, ISBN: 9789354992162
- Zen in the Art of Archery by Eugen Herrigel, ISBN: 9789354991059

Search the book by its ISBN

Contents

Chapter 1

Salaam

The Western student is apt to be somewhat confused in his ideas regarding the Yogis and their philosophy and practice. Travelers to India have written great tales about the hordes of fakirs, mendicants and mountebanks who infest the great roads of India and the streets of its cities, and who impudently claim the title "Yogi." The Western student is scarcely to be blamed for thinking of the typical Yogi as an emaciated, fanatical, dirty, ignorant Hindu, who either sits in a fixed posture until his body becomes ossified, or else holds his arm up in the air until it becomes stiff and withered and forever after remains in that position, or perhaps clenches his fist and holds it tight until his fingernails grow through the palms of his hands. That these people exist is true, but their claim to the title "Yogi" seems as absurd to the true Yogi as does the claim to the title "Doctor" on the part of the man who pares one's corns seem to the eminent surgeon, or as does the title of "Professor," as assumed by the street corner vendor of worm medicine, seem to the President of Harvard or Yale.

There have been for ages past in India and other Oriental countries men who devoted their time and attention to the development of Man, physically, mentally and spiritually. The experience of generations of earnest seekers has been handed down for centuries from teacher to pupil, and gradually a definite Yogi science was built up. To these investigations and teachings was finally applied the term "Yogi," from the Sanskrit word "Yug," meaning "to join." From the same source comes the English word "yoke," with a similar meaning. Its use in connection with these teachings is difficult to trace, different authorities giving different explanations, but probably the most ingenious is that which holds that it is intended as the Hindu equivalent for the idea conveyed by the English phrase, "getting into harness," or "yoking up," as the Yogi undoubtedly "gets into harness" in his work of controlling the body and mind by the Will.

Yoga is divided into several branches, ranging from that which teaches the control of the body, to that which teaches the attainment of the highest spiritual development. In the work we will not go into the higher phases of the subject, except when the "Science of Breath" touches upon the same. The "Science of Breath" touches Yoga at many points, and although chiefly concerned with the development and control of the physical, has also its psychic side, and even enters the field of spiritual development.

In India there are great schools of Yoga, comprising thousands of the leading minds of that great country. The Yoga philosophy is the rule of life for many people. The pure Yogi teachings, however, are given only to the few, the masses being satisfied with the crumbs which fall from the tables of the educated classes, the Oriental custom in this respect being opposed to that of the Western world. But Western ideas are beginning to have their effect even in the Orient, and teachings which were once given only to the few are now freely offered to any who are ready to receive them. The East and the West are growing closer together, and both are profiting by the close contact, each influencing the other.

The Hindu Yogis have always paid great attention to the Science of Breath, for reasons which will be apparent to the student who reads this book. Many Western writers have touched upon this phase of the Yogi teachings, but we believe that it has been reserved for the writer of this work to give to the Western student, in concise form and simple language, the underlying principles of the Yogi Science of Breath, together with many of the favorite Yogi breathing exercises and methods. We have given the Western idea as well as the Oriental, showing how one dovetails into the other. We have used the ordinary English terms, almost entirely, avoiding the Sanskrit terms, so confusing to the average Western reader.

The first part of the book is devoted to the physical phase of the Science of Breath; then the psychic and mental sides are considered, and finally the spiritual side is touched upon.

We may be pardoned if we express ourselves as pleased with our success in condensing so much Yogi lore into so few pages, and by the use of words and terms which may be understood by anyone. Our only fear is that it's very simplicity may cause some to pass it by as unworthy of attention, while they pass on their way searching for something "deep," mysterious and non-understandable. However, the Western mind is eminently practical, and we know that it is only a question of a short time before it will recognize the practicability of this work.

We greet our students, with our most profound salaam, and bid them be seated for their first lessons in the Yogi Science of Breath.

Chapter 2

Breath is Life

Life is absolutely dependent upon the act of breathing. "Breath is Life."

Differ as they may upon details of theory and terminology, the Oriental and the Occidental agree upon these fundamental principles.

To breathe is to live, and without breath there is no life. Not only are the higher animals dependent upon breath for life and health, but even the lower forms of animal life must breathe to live, and plant life is likewise dependent upon the air for continued existence.

The infant draws in a long, deep breath, retains it for a moment to extract from it its life-giving properties, and then exhales it in a long wail, and lo! its life upon earth has begun. The old man gives a faint gasp, ceases to breathe, and life is over. From the first faint breath of the infant to the last gasp of the dying man, it is one long story of continued breathing. Life is but a series of breaths.

Breathing may be considered the most important of all of the functions of the body, for, indeed, all the other functions depend upon it. Man may exist some time without eating; a shorter time without drinking; but without breathing his existence may be measured by a few minutes.

And not only is Man dependent upon Breath for life, but he is largely dependent upon correct habits of breathing for continued vitality and freedom from disease. An intelligent control of our breathing power will lengthen our days upon earth by giving us increased vitality and powers of resistance, and, on the other hand, unintelligent and careless breathing will tend to shorten our days, by decreasing our vitality and laying us open to disease.

Man in his normal state had no need of instruction in breathing. Like the lower animal and the child, he breathed naturally and properly, as nature intended him to do, but civilization has changed him in this and other respects. He has contracted improper methods and attitudes of walking, standing and sitting, which have robbed him of his birthright of natural and correct breathing. He has paid a high price for civilization. The savage, to-day, breathes naturally, unless he has been contaminated by the habits of civilized man.

The percentage of civilized men who breathe correctly is quite small, and the result is shown in contracted chests and stooping shoulders, and the terrible increase in diseases of the respiratory organs, including that dread monster, Consumption, "the white scourge." Eminent authorities have stated that one generation of correct breathers would regenerate the race, and disease would be so rare as to be looked upon as a curiosity. Whether looked at from the standpoint of the Oriental or Occidental, the connection between correct breathing and health is readily seen and explained.

The Occidental teachings show that the physical health depends very materially upon correct breathing. The Oriental teachers not only admit that their Occidental brothers are right, but say that in addition to the physical benefit derived from correct habits of breathing, Man's mental power, happiness, self-control, clear-sightedness, morals, and even his spiritual growth may be increased by an understanding of the "Science of Breath." Whole schools of Oriental Philosophy have been founded upon this science, and this knowledge when grasped by the Western races, and by them put to the practical use which is their strong point, will work wonders among them. The theory of the East, wedded to the practice of the West, will produce worthy offspring.

This work will take up the Yogi "Science of Breath," which includes not only all that is known to the Western physiologist and hygienist, but the occult side of the subject as well. It not only points out the way to physical health along the lines of what Western scientists have termed "deep breathing," etc., but also goes into the less known phases of the subject, and shows how the Hindu Yogi controls his body, increasing his mental capacity, and develops the spiritual side of his nature by the "Science of Breath."

The Yogi practices exercises by which he attains control of his body, and is enabled to send to any organ or part an increased flow of vital force or "prana," thereby strengthening and invigorating the part or organ. He knows all that his Western scientific brother knows about the physiological effect of correct breathing, but he also knows that the air contains more than oxygen and hydrogen and nitrogen, and that something more is accomplished than the mere oxygenating of the blood. He knows something about "prana," of which his Western brother is ignorant, and he is fully aware of the nature and manner of handling that great principle of energy, and is fully informed as to its effect upon the human body and mind. He knows that by rhythmical breathing one may bring himself into harmonious vibration with nature, and aid in the unfoldment of his latent powers. He knows that by controlled breathing he may not only cure disease in himself and others, but also practically do away with fear and worry and the baser emotions.

To teach these things is the object of this work. We will give in a few chapters concise explanations and instructions, which might be extended into volumes. We hope to awaken the minds of the Western world to the value of the Yogi "Science of Breath."

Chapter 3

The Exoteric Theory of Breath

In this chapter we will give you briefly the theories of the Western scientific world regarding the functions of the respiratory organs, and the part in the human economy played by the breath. In subsequent chapters we will give the additional theories and ascertained facts of the Oriental school of thought and research. The Oriental accepts the theories and facts of his Western brothers (which have been known to him for centuries) and adds thereto much that the latter do not now accept, but which they will in due time "discover" and which, after renaming, they will present to the world as a great truth.

Before taking up the Western idea, it will perhaps be better to give a hasty general idea of the Organs of Respiration.

The Organs of Respiration consist of the lungs and the air passages leading to them. The lungs are two in number, and occupy the pleural chamber of the thorax, one on each side of the median line, being separated from each other by the heart, the greater blood vessels and the larger air tubes. Each lung is free in all directions, except at the root, which consists chiefly of the bronchi, arteries and veins connecting the lungs with the trachea and heart. The lungs are spongy and porous, and their tissues are very elastic. They are covered with a delicately constructed but strong sac, known as the pleural sac, one wall of which closely adheres to the lung, and the other to the inner wall of the chest, and which secretes a fluid which allows the inner surfaces of the walls to glide easily upon each other in the act of breathing.

The Air Passages consist of the interior of the nose, pharynx, larynx, windpipe or trachea, and the bronchial tubes. When we breathe, we draw in the air through the nose, in which it is warmed by contact with the mucous membrane, which is richly supplied with blood, and after it has passed through the pharynx and larynx it passes into the trachea or windpipe, which subdivides into numerous tubes called the bronchial tubes (bronchia), which in turn subdivide into and terminate in minute subdivisions in all the small air spaces in the lungs, of which the lungs contain millions. A writer has stated that if the air cells of the lungs were spread out over an unbroken surface, they would cover an area of fourteen thousand square feet.

The air is drawn into the lungs by the action of the diaphragm, a great, strong, flat, sheet-like muscle, stretched across the chest, separating the chest-box from the abdomen. The diaphragm's action is almost as automatic as that of the heart, although it may be transformed into a semi-voluntary muscle by an effort of the will. When it expands, it increases the size of the chest and lungs, and the air rushes into the vacuum thus created. When it relaxes the chest and lungs contract and the air is expelled from the lungs.

Now, before considering what happens to the air in the lungs, let us look a little into the matter of the circulation of the blood. The blood, as you know, is driven by the heart, through the arteries, into the capillaries, thus reaching every part of the body, which it vitalizes, nourishes and strengthens. It then returns by means of the capillaries by another route, the veins, to the heart, from whence it is drawn to the lungs.

The blood starts on its arterial journey, bright red and rich, laden with life-giving qualities and properties. It returns by the venous route, poor, blue and dull, being laden down with the waste matter of the system. It goes out like a fresh stream from the mountains; it returns as a stream of sewer water. This foul stream goes to the right auricle of the heart. When this auricle becomes filled, it contracts and forces the stream of blood through an opening in the right ventricle of the heart, which in turn sends it on to the lungs, where it is distributed by millions of hair-like blood vessels to the air cells of the lungs, of which we have spoken. Now, let us take up the story of the lungs at this point.

The foul stream of blood is now distributed among the millions of tiny air cells in the lungs. A breath of air is inhaled and the oxygen of the air comes in contact with the impure blood through the thin walls of the hair-like blood vessels of the lungs, which walls are thick enough to hold the blood, but thin enough to admit the oxygen to penetrate them. When the oxygen comes in contact with the blood, a form of combustion takes place, and the blood takes up oxygen and releases carbonic acid gas generated from the waste products and poisonous matter which has been gathered up by the blood from all parts of the system.

The blood thus purified and oxygenated is carried back to the heart, again rich, red and bright, and laden with life-giving properties and qualities. Upon reaching the left auricle of the heart, it is forced into the left ventricle, from whence it is again forced out through the arteries on its mission of life to all parts of the system. It is estimated that in a single day of twenty-four hours, 35,000 pints of blood traverse the capillaries of the lungs, the blood corpuscles passing in single file and being exposed to the oxygen of the air on both of their surfaces. When one considers the minute details of the process alluded to, he is lost in wonder and admiration at Nature's infinite care and intelligence.

It will be seen that unless fresh air in sufficient quantities reaches the lungs, the foul stream of venous blood cannot be purified, and consequently not only is the body thus robbed of nourishment, but the waste products which should have been destroyed are returned to the circulation and poison the system, and death ensues. Impure air acts in the same way, only in a lessened degree. It will also be seen that if one does not breathe in a sufficient quantity of air, the work of the blood cannot go on properly, and the result is that the body is insufficiently nourished and disease ensues, or a state of imperfect health is experienced. The blood of one who breathes improperly is, of course, of a bluish, dark color, lacking the rich redness of pure arterial blood. This often shows itself in a poor complexion. Proper breathing, and a consequent good circulation, results in a clear, bright complexion.

A little reflection will show the vital importance of correct breathing. If the blood is not fully purified by the regenerative process of the lungs, it returns to the arteries in an abnormal state, insufficiently purified and imperfectly cleansed of the impurities which it took up on its return journey. These impurities if returned to the system will certainly manifest in some form of disease, either in a form of blood disease or some disease resulting from impaired functioning of some insufficiently nourished organ or tissue.

The blood, when properly exposed to the air in the lungs, not only has its impurities consumed, and parts with its noxious carbonic acid gas, but it also takes up and absorbs a certain quantity of oxygen which it carries to all parts of the body, where it is needed in order that Nature may perform her processes properly. When the oxygen comes in contact with the blood, it unites with the hemoglobin of the blood and is carried to every cell, tissue, muscle and organ, which it invigorates and strengthens, replacing the worn out cells and tissue by new materials which Nature converts to her use. Arterial blood, properly exposed to the air, contains about 25 per cent of free oxygen.

Not only is every part vitalized by the oxygen, but the act of digestion depends materially upon a certain amount of oxygenation of the food, and this can be accomplished only by the oxygen in the blood coming in contact with the food and producing a certain form of combustion. It is therefore necessary that a proper supply of oxygen be taken through the lungs. This accounts for the fact that weak lungs and poor digestion are so often found together. To grasp the full significance of this statement, one must remember that the entire body receives nourishment from the food assimilated, and that imperfect assimilation always means an imperfectly nourished body. Even the lungs themselves depend upon the same source for nourishment, and if through imperfect breathing the assimilation becomes imperfect, and the lungs in turn become weakened, they are rendered still less able to perform their work properly, and so in turn the body becomes further weakened. Every particle of food and drink must be oxygenated before it can yield us the proper nourishment, and before the waste products of the system can be reduced to the proper condition to be eliminated from the system. Lack of sufficient oxygen means Imperfect nutrition, Imperfect elimination and imperfect health. Verily, "breath is life."

The combustion arising from the change in the waste products generates heat and equalizes the temperature of the body. Good breathers are not apt to "take cold," and they generally have plenty of good warm blood which enables them to resist the changes in the outer temperature.

In addition to the above-mentioned important processes the act of breathing gives exercise to the internal organs and muscles, which feature is generally overlooked by the Western writers on the subject, but which the Yogis fully appreciate.

In imperfect or shallow breathing, only a portion of the lung cells are brought into play, and a great portion of the lung capacity is lost, the system suffering in proportion to the amount of under-oxygenation. The lower animals, in their native state, breathe naturally, and primitive man undoubtedly did the same. The abnormal manner of living adopted by civilized man—the shadow that follows upon civilization—has robbed us of our natural habit of breathing, and the race has greatly suffered thereby. Man's only physical salvation is to "get back to Nature."

Chapter 4

The Esoteric Theory of Breath

The Science of Breath, like many other teachings, has its esoteric or inner phase, as well as its exoteric or external. The physiological phase may be termed the outer or exoteric side of the subject, and the phase which we will now consider may be termed its esoteric or inner side. Occultists, in all ages and lands, have always taught, usually secretly to a few followers, that there was to be found in the air a substance or principle from which all activity, vitality and life was derived. They differed in their terms and names for this force, as well as in the details of the theory, but the main principle is to be found in all occult teachings and philosophies, and has for centuries formed a portion of the teachings of the Oriental Yogis.

In order to avoid misconceptions arising from the various theories regarding this great principle, which theories are usually attached to some name given the principle, we, in this work, will speak of the principle as "Prana," this word being the Sanskrit term meaning "Absolute Energy." Many occult authorities teach that the principle which the Hindus term "Prana" is the universal principle of energy or force, and that all energy or force is derived from that principle, or, rather, is a particular form of manifestation of that principle. These theories do not concern us in the consideration of the subject matter of this work, and we will therefore confine ourselves to an understanding of prana as the principle of energy exhibited in all living things, which distinguishes them from a lifeless thing. We may consider it as the active principle of life—Vital Force, if you please. It is found in all forms of life, from the amoeba to man—from the most elementary form of plant life to the highest form of animal life. Prana is all pervading. It is found in all things having life, and as the occult philosophy teaches that life is in all things—in every atom—the apparent lifelessness of some things being only a lesser degree of manifestation, we may understand their teachings that prana is everywhere, in everything. Prana must not be confounded with the Ego—that bit of Divine Spirit in every soul, around which clusters matter and energy. Prana is merely a form of energy used by the Ego in its material manifestation. When the Ego leaves the body, the prana, being no longer under its control, responds only to the orders of the individual atoms, or groups of atoms, forming the body, and as the body disintegrates and is resolved to its original elements, each atom takes with it sufficient prana to enable it to form new combinations, the unused prana returning to the great universal storehouse from which it came. With the Ego in control, cohesion exists and the atoms are held together by the Will of the Ego.

Prana is the name by which we designate a universal principle, which principle is the essence of all motion, force or energy, whether manifested in gravitation, electricity, the revolution of the planets, and all forms of life, from the highest to the lowest. It may be called the soul of Force and Energy in all their forms, and that principle which, operating in a certain way, causes that form of activity which accompanies Life.

This great principle is in all forms of matter, and yet it is not matter. It is in the air, but it is not the air nor one of its chemical constituents. Animal and plant life breathe it in with the air, and yet if the air contained it not they would die even though they might be filled with air. It is taken up by the system along with the oxygen, and yet is not the oxygen. The Hebrew writer of the book of Genesis knew the difference between the atmospheric air and the mysterious and potent principle contained within it. He speaks of neshemetruach-chayim, which, translated, means "the breath of the spirit of life." In the Hebrew neshemet means the ordinary breath of atmospheric air, and chayim means life or lives, while the word ruach means the "spirit of life," which occultists claim is the same principle which we speak of as Prana.

Prana is in the atmospheric air, but it is also elsewhere, and it penetrates where the air cannot reach. The oxygen in the air plays an important part in sustaining animal life, and the carbon plays a similar part with plant life, but Prana has its own distinct part to play in the manifestation of life, aside from the physiological functions.

We are constantly inhaling the air charged with prana, and are as constantly extracting the latter from the air and appropriating it to our uses. Prana is found in its freest state in the atmospheric air, which when fresh is fairly charged with it, and we draw it to us more easily from the air than from any other source. In ordinary breathing we absorb and extract a normal supply of prana, but by controlled and regulated breathing (generally known as Yogi breathing) we are enabled to extract a greater supply, which is stored away in the brain and nerve centers, to be used when necessary. We may store away prana, just as the storage battery stores away electricity. The many powers attributed to advanced occultists is due largely to their knowledge of this fact and their intelligent use of this stored-up energy. The Yogis know that by certain forms of breathing they establish certain relations with the supply of prana and may draw on the same for what they require. Not only do they strengthen all parts of their body in this way, but the brain itself may receive increased energy from the same source, and latent faculties be developed and psychic powers attained. One who has mastered the science of storing away prana, either consciously or unconsciously, often radiates vitality and strength which is felt by those coming in contact with him, and such a person may impart this strength to others, and give them increased vitality and health. What is called "magnetic healing" is performed in this way, although many practitioners are not aware of the source of their power.

Western scientists have been dimly aware of this great principle with which the air is charged, but finding that they could find no chemical trace of it, or make it register an any of their instruments, they have generally treated the Oriental theory with disdain. They could not explain this principle, and so denied it. They seem, however, to recognize that the air in certain places possesses a greater amount of "something" and sick people are directed by their physicians to seek such places in hopes of regaining, lost health.

The oxygen in the air is appropriated by the blood and is made use of by the circulatory system. The prana in the air is appropriated by the nervous system, and is used in its work. And as the oxygenated blood is carried to all parts of the system, building up and replenishing, so is the prana carried to all parts of the nervous system, adding strength and vitality. If we think of prana as being the active principle of what we call "vitality," we will be able to form a much clearer idea of what an important part it plays in our lives. Just as is the oxygen in the blood used up by the wants of the system, so the supply of prana taken up by the nervous system is exhausted by our thinking, willing, acting, etc., and in consequence constant replenishing is necessary. Every thought, every act, every effort of the will, every motion of a muscle, uses up a certain amount of what we call nerve force, which is really a form of prana. To move a muscle the brain sends out an impulse over the nerves, and the muscle contracts, and so much prana is expended. When it is remembered that the greater portion of prana acquired by man comes to him from the air inhaled, the importance of proper breathing is readily understood.

Chapter 5

The Nervous System

It will be noticed that the Western scientific theories regarding the breath confine themselves to the effects of the absorption of oxygen, and its use through the circulatory system, while the Yogi theory also takes into consideration the absorption of Prana, and its manifestation through the channels of the Nervous System. Before proceeding further, it may be as well to take a hasty glance at the Nervous System.

The Nervous System of man is divided into two great systems, viz., the Cerebro-Spinal System and the Sympathetic System. The Cerebro-Spinal System consists of all that part of the Nervous System contained within the cranial cavity and the spinal canal, viz., the brain and the spinal cord, together with the nerves which branch off from the same. This system presides over the functions of animal life known as volition, sensation, etc. The Sympathetic System includes all that part of the Nervous System located principally in the thoracic, abdominal and pelvic cavities, and which is distributed to the internal organs. It has control over the involuntary processes, such as growth, nutrition, etc.

The Cerebro-Spinal System attends to all the seeing, hearing, tasting, smelling, feeling, etc. It sets things in motion; it is used by the Ego to think—to manifest consciousness. It is the instrument with which the Ego communicates with the outside world. This system may be likened to a telephone system, with the brain as the central office, and the spinal column and nerves as cable and wires respectively.

The brain is a great mass of nerve tissue, and consists of three parts, viz., the Cerebrum or brain proper, which occupies the upper, front, middle and back portion of the skull; the Cerebellum, or "little brain," which fills the lower and back portion of the skull; and the Medulla Oblongata, which Is the broadened commencement of the spinal cord, lying before and in front of the Cerebellum.

The Cerebrum is the organ of that part of the mind which manifests itself in intellectual action. The Cerebellum regulates the movements of the voluntary muscles. The Medulla Oblongata is the upper enlarged end of the spinal cord, and from it and the Cerebrum branch forth the Cranial Nerves which reach to various parts of the head, to the organs of special sense, and to some of the thoracic and abdominal organs, and to the organs of respiration.

The Spinal Cord, or spinal marrow, fills the spinal canal in the vertebral column, or "backbone." It is a long mass of nerve tissue, branching off at the several vertebrae to nerves communicating with all parts of the body. The Spinal Cord is like a large telephone cable, and the emerging nerves are like the private wires connecting therewith.

The Sympathetic Nervous System consists of a double chain of Ganglia on the side of the Spinal column, and scattered ganglia in the head, neck, chest and abdomen. (A ganglion is a mass of nervous matter including nerve cells.) These ganglia are connected with each other by filaments, and are also connected with the Cerebro-Spinal System by motor and sensory nerves. From these ganglia numerous fibers branch out to the organs of the body, blood vessels, etc. At various points, the nerves meet together and form what are known as plexuses. The Sympathetic System practically controls the involuntary processes, such as circulation, respiration and digestion.

The power or force transmitted from the brain to all parts of the body by means of the nerves, is known to Western science as "nerve force," although the Yogi knows it to be a manifestation of Prana. In character and rapidity it resembles the electric current. It will be seen that without this "nerve force" the heart cannot beat; the blood cannot circulate; the lungs cannot breathe; the various organs cannot function; in fact the machinery of the body comes to a stop without it. Nay more, even the brain cannot think without Prana be present. When these facts are considered, the importance of the absorption of Prana must be evident to all, and the Science of Breath assumes an importance even greater than that accorded it by Western science.

The Yogi teachings go further than does Western science, in one important feature of the Nervous System. We allude to what Western science terms the "Solar Plexus," and which it considers as merely one of a series of certain matted nets of sympathetic nerves with their ganglia found in various parts of the body. Yogi science teaches that this Solar Plexus is really a most important part of the Nervous System, and that it is a form of brain, playing one of the principal parts in the human economy. Western science seems to be moving gradually towards a recognition of this fact which has been known to the Yogis of the East for centuries, and some recent Western writers have termed the Solar Plexus the "Abdominal Brain." The Solar Plexus is situated in the Epigastric region, just back of the "pit of the stomach" on either side of the spinal column. It is composed of white and gray brain matter, similar to that composing the other brains of man. It has control of the main internal organs of man, and plays a much more important part than is generally recognized. We will not go into the Yogi theory regarding the Solar Plexus, further than to say that they know it as the great central store-house of Prana. Men have been known to be instantly killed by a severe blow over the Solar Plexus, and prize fighters recognize its vulnerability and frequently temporarily paralyze their opponents by a blow over this region.

The name "Solar" is well bestowed on this "brain," as it radiates strength and energy to all parts of the body, even the upper brains depending largely upon it as a storehouse of Prana. Sooner or later Western science will fully recognize the real function of the Solar Plexus, and will accord to it a far more important place then it now occupies in their text-books and teachings.

Chapter 6

Nostril-Breathing vs. Mouth-Breathing

One of the first lessons in the Yogi Science of Breath, Is to learn how to breathe through the nostrils, and to overcome the common practice of mouth-breathing.

The breathing mechanism of Man is so constructed that he may breathe either through the mouth or nasal tubes, but it is a matter of vital importance to him which method he follows, as one brings health and strength and the other disease and weakness.

It should not be necessary to state to the student that the proper method of breathing is to take the breath through the nostrils, but alas! the ignorance among civilized people regarding this simple matter is astounding. We find people in all walks of life habitually breathing through their mouths, and allowing their children to follow their horrible and disgusting example.

Many of the diseases to which civilized man is subject are undoubtedly caused by this common habit of mouth-breathing. Children permitted to breathe in this way grow up with impaired vitality and weakened constitutions, and in manhood and womanhood break down and become chronic invalids. The mother of the savage race does better, being evidently guided by her intuition. She seems to instinctively recognize that the nostrils are the proper channels for the conveyal of air to the lungs, and she trains her infant to close its little lips and breathe through the nose. She tips its head forward when it is asleep, which attitude closes the lips and makes nostril-breathing imperative. If our civilized mothers were to adopt the same plan, it would work a great good for the race.

Many contagious diseases are contracted by the disgusting habit of mouth-breathing, and many cases of cold and catarrhal affections are also attributable to the same cause. Many persons who, for the sake of appearances, keep their mouth closed during the day, persist in mouth-breathing at night and often contract disease in this way.

Carefully conducted scientific experiments have shown that soldiers and sailors who sleep with their mouths open are much more liable to contract contagious diseases than those who breathe properly through the nostrils. An instance is related in which small-pox became epidemic on a man-of-war in foreign parts, and every death which resulted was that of some sailor or marine who was a mouth-breather, not a single nostril-breather succumbing.

The organs of respiration have their only protective apparatus, filter, or dust-catcher, in the nostrils. When the breath is taken through the mouth, there is nothing from mouth to lungs to strain the air, or to catch the dust and other foreign matter in the air. From mouth to lungs the dirt or impure substance has a clear track, and the entire respiratory system is unprotected. And, moreover, such incorrect breathing admits cold air to the organs, thereby injuring them. Inflammation of the respiratory organs often results from the inhalation of cold air through the mouth. The man who breathes through the mouth at night, always awakens with a parched feeling in the mouth and a dryness in the throat. He is violating one of nature's laws, and is sowing the seeds of disease.

Once more, remember that the mouth affords no protection to the respiratory organs, and cold air, dust and impurities and germs readily enter by that door. On the other hand, the nostrils and nasal passages show evidence of the careful design of nature in this respect. The nostrils are two narrow, tortuous channels, containing numerous bristly hairs which serve the purpose of a filter or sieve to strain the air of its impurities, etc., which are expelled when the breath is exhaled. Not only do the nostrils serve this important purpose, but they also perform an important function in warming the air inhaled. The long narrow winding nostrils are filled with warm mucous membrane, which coming in contact with the inhaled air Warms it so that it can do no damage to the delicate organs of the throat, or to the lungs.

No animal, excepting man, sleeps with the mouth open or breathes through the mouth, and in fact it is believed that it is only civilized man who so perverts nature's functions, as the savage and barbarian races almost invariably breathe correctly. It is probable that this unnatural habit among civilized men has been acquired through unnatural methods of living, enervating luxuries and excessive warmth.

The refining, filtering and straining apparatus of the nostrils renders the air fit to reach the delicate organs of the throat and the lungs, and the air is not fit to so reach these organs until it has passed through nature's refining process. The impurities which are stopped and retained by the sieves and mucous membrane of the nostrils, are thrown out again by the expelled breath, in exhalation, and in case they have accumulated too rapidly or have managed to escape through the sieves and have penetrated forbidden regions, nature protects us by producing a sneeze which violently ejects the intruder.

The air, when it enters the lungs is as different from the outside air, as is distilled water different from the water of the cistern. The intricate purifying organization of the nostrils, arresting and holding the impure particles in the air, is as important as is the action of the mouth in stopping cherry-stones and fish-bones and preventing them from being carried on to the stomach. Man should no more breathe through his mouth than he would attempt to take food through his nose.

Another feature of mouth-breathing is that the nasal passages, being thus comparatively unused, consequently fail to keep themselves clean and clear, and become clogged up and unclean, and are apt to contract local diseases. Like abandoned roads that soon become filled with weeds and rubbish, unused nostrils become filled with impurities and foul matter.

One who habitually breathes through the nostrils is not likely to be troubled with clogged or stuffy nostrils, but for the benefit of those who have been more or less addicted to the unnatural mouth-breathing, and who wish to acquire the natural and rational method, it may perhaps be well to add a few words regarding the way to keep their nostrils clean and free from impurities.

A favorite Oriental method is to snuff a little water up the nostrils allowing it to run down the passage into the throat, from thence it may be ejected through the mouth. Some Hindu yogis immerse the face in a bowl of water, and by a sort of suction draw in quite a quantity of water, but this latter method requires considerable practice, and the first mentioned method is equally efficacious, and much more easily performed.

Another good plan is to open the window and breathe freely, closing one nostril with the finger or thumb, sniffing up the air through the open nostril. Then repeat the process on the other nostril. Repeat several times, changing nostrils. This method will usually clear the nostrils of obstructions.

In case the trouble is caused by catarrh it is well to apply a little vaseline or camphor ice or similar preparation. Or sniff up a little witch-hazel extract once in a while, and you will notice a marked improvement. A little care and attention will result in the nostrils becoming clean and remaining so.

We have given considerable space to this subject of nostril-breathing, not only because of its great importance in its reference to health, but because nostril-breathing is a prerequisite to the practice of the breathing exercises to be given later in this book, and because nostril-breathing is one of the basic principles underlying the Yogi Science of Breath.

We urge upon the student the necessity of acquiring this method of breathing if he has it not, and caution him against dismissing this phase of the subject as unimportant.

Chapter 7

Four Methods of Respiration

In the consideration of the question of respiration, we must begin by considering the mechanical arrangements whereby the respiratory movements are effected. The mechanics of respiration manifest through (1) the elastic movements of the lungs, and (2) the activities of the sides and bottom of the thoracic cavity in which the lungs are contained. The thorax is that portion of the trunk between the neck and the abdomen, the cavity of which (known as the thoracic cavity) is occupied mainly by the lungs and heart. It is bounded by the spinal column, the ribs with their cartilages, the breastbone, and below by the diaphragm. It is generally spoken of as "the chest." It has been compared to a completely shut, conical box, the small end of which Is turned upward, the back of the box being formed by the spinal column, the front by the breastbone and the sides by the ribs.

The ribs are twenty-four in number, twelve on each side, and emerge from each side of the spinal column. The upper seven pair are known as "true ribs," being fastened to the breastbone direct, while the lower five pairs are called (false ribs) or "floating ribs," because they are not so fastened, the upper two of them being fastened by cartilage to the other ribs, the remainder having no cartilages, their forward ends being free.

The ribs are moved in respiration by two superficial muscular layers, known as the intercostal muscles. The diaphragm, the muscular partition before alluded to, separates the chest box from the abdominal cavity.

In the act of inhalation the muscles expand the lungs so that a vacuum is created and the air rushes in accordance with the well known law of physics. Everything depends upon the muscles concerned in the process of respiration, which we may as, for convenience, term the "respiratory muscles." Without the aid of these muscles the lungs cannot expand, and upon the proper use and control of these muscles the Science of Breath largely depends. The proper control of these muscles will result in the ability to attain the maximum degree of lung expansion, and the greatest amount of the life giving properties of the air into the system.

The Yogis classify Respiration into four general methods, viz:

1. High Breathing.
2. Mid Breathing.
3. Low Breathing.
4. Yogi Complete Breathing.

We will give a general idea of the first three methods, and a more extended treatment of the fourth method, upon which the Yogi Science of Breath is largely based.

1. High Breathing

This form of breathing is known to the Western world as Clavicular Breathing, or Collarbone Breathing. One breathing in this way elevates the ribs and raises the collarbone and shoulders, at the same time drawing in the abdomen and pushing its contents up against the diaphragm, which in turn is raised.

The upper part of the chest and lungs, which is the smallest, is used, and consequently but a minimum amount of air enters the lungs. In addition to this, the diaphragm being raised, there can be no expansion in that direction. A study of the anatomy of the chest will convince any student that in this way a maximum amount of effort is used to obtain a minimum amount of benefit.

High Breathing is probably the worst form of breathing known to man and requires the greatest expenditure of energy with the smallest amount of benefit. It is an energy-wasting, poor-returns plan. It is quite common among the Western races, many women being addicted to It, and even singers, clergymen, lawyers and others, who should know better, using it ignorantly.

Many diseases of the vocal organs and organs of respiration may be directly traced to this barbarous method of breathing, and the straining of delicate organs caused by this method, often results in the harsh, disagreeable voices heard on all sides. Many persons who breathe In this way become addicted to the disgusting practice of "mouth-breathing" described in a preceding chapter.

If the student has any doubts about what has been said regarding this form of breathing, let him try the experiment of expelling all the air from his lungs, then standing erect, with hands at sides, let him raise the shoulders and collar-bone and inhale. He will find that the amount of air inhaled far below normal. Then let him inhale a full breath, after dropping the shoulders and collar-bone, and he will receive an object lesson in breathing which he will be apt to remember much longer than he would any words, printed or spoken.

2. Mid Breathing

This method of respiration is known to Western students as Rib Breathing, or Inter-Costal Breathing, and while less objectionable than High Breathing, is far inferior to either Low Breathing or to the Yogi Complete Breath. In Mid Breathing the diaphragm is pushed upward, and the abdomen drawn in. The ribs are raised somewhat, and the chest is partially expanded. It is quite common among men who have made no study of the subject. As there are two better methods known, we give it only passing notice, and that principally to call your attention to its short-comings.

3. Low Breathing

This form of respiration is far better than either of the two preceding forms: and of recent years many Western writers have extolled its merits, and have exploited it under the names of "Abdominal Breathing," "Deep Breathing," "Diaphragmatic Breathing," etc., etc., and much good has been accomplished by the attention of the public having been directed to the subject, and many having been Induced to substitute it for the interior and injurious methods above alluded to. Many "systems" of breathing have been built around Low Breathing, and students have paid high prices to learn the new (?) systems. But, as we have said, much good has resulted, and after all the students who paid high prices to learn revamped old systems undoubtedly got their money's worth if they were Induced to discard the old methods of High Breathing and Low Breathing.

Although many Western authorities write and speak of this method as the best known form of breathing, the Yogis know it to be but a part of a system which they have used for centuries and which they know as "The Complete Breath." It must be admitted, however, that one must be acquainted with the principles of Low Breathing before he can grasp the idea of Complete Breathing.

Let us again consider the diaphragm. What is it? We have seen that it is the great partition muscle, which separates the chest and its contents from the abdomen and its contents. When at rest it presents a concave surface to the abdomen. That is, the diaphragm as viewed from the abdomen would seem like the sky as viewed from the earth—the interior of an arched surface. Consequently the side of the diaphragm toward the chest organs is like a protruding rounded surface—like a hill. When the diaphragm is brought into use the hill formation is lowered and the diaphragm presses upon the abdominal organs and forces out the abdomen.

In Low Breathing, the lungs are given freer play than in the methods already mentioned, and consequently more air is inhaled. This fact has led the majority of Western writers to speak and write of Low Breathing (which they call Abdominal Breathing) as the highest and best method known to science. But the Oriental Yogi has long known of a better method, and some few Western writers have also recognized this fact. The trouble with all methods of breathing, other than "Yogi Complete Breathing" is that in none of these methods do the lungs become filled with air—at the best only a portion of the lung space is filled, even in Low Breathing. High Breathing fills only the upper portion of the lungs. Mid Breathing fills only the middle and a portion of the upper parts. Low Breathing fills only the lower and middle parts. It is evident that any method that fills the entire lung space must be far preferable to those filling only certain parts Any method which will fill the entire lung space must be the greatest value to Man in the way of allowing him to absorb the greatest quantity of oxygen and to store away the greatest amount of prana. The Complete Breath is known to the Yogis to be the best method of respiration known to science.

The Yogi Complete Breath

Yogi Complete Breathing includes all the good points of High Breathing, Mid Breathing and Low Breathing, with the objectionable features of each eliminated. It brings into play the entire respiratory apparatus, every part of the lungs, every air-cell, every respiratory muscle. The entire respiratory organism responds to this method of breathing, and the maximum amount of benefit is derived from the minimum expenditure of energy. The chest cavity is increased to its normal limits in all directions and every part of the machinery performs its natural work and functions.

One of the most important features of this method of breathing is the fact that the respiratory muscles are fully called into play, whereas in the other forms of breathing only a portion of these muscles are so used. In Complete Breathing, among other muscles, those controlling the ribs are actively used, which increases the space in which the lungs may expand, and also gives the proper support to the organs when needed, Nature availing herself of the perfection of the principle of leverage in this process. Certain muscles hold the lower ribs firmly in position, while other muscles bend them outward.

Then again, in this method, the diaphragm is under perfect control and is able to perform its functions properly, and in such manner as to yield the maximum degree of service.

In the rib-action, above alluded to, the lower ribs are controlled by the diaphragm which draws them slightly downward, while other muscles hold them in place and the intercostal muscles force them outward, which combined action increases the mid-chest cavity to its maximum. In addition to this muscular action, the upper ribs are also lifted and forced outward by the intercostal muscles, which increases the capacity of the upper chest to its fullest extent.

If you have studied the special features of the four given methods of breathing, you will at once see that the Complete Breath comprises all the advantageous features of the three other methods, plus the reciprocal advantages accruing from the combined action of the high-chest, mid-chest, and diaphragmatic regions, and the normal rhythm thus obtained.

In our next chapter, we will take up the Complete Breath in practice, and will give full directions for the acquirement of this superior method of breathing, with exercises, etc.

Chapter 8

How to Acquire the Yogi Complete Breath

The Yogi Complete Breath is the fundamental breath of the entire Yogi Science of Breath, and the student must fully acquaint himself with it, and master it perfectly before he can hope to obtain results from the other forms of breath-mentioned and given in this book. He should not be content with half-learning it, but should go to work in earnest until it becomes his natural method of breathing. This will require work, time and patience, but without these things nothing is ever accomplished. There is no royal road to the Science of Breath, and the student must be prepared to practice and study in earnest if he expect to receive results. The results obtained by a complete mastery of the Science of Breath are great, and no one who has attained them would willingly go back to the old methods, and he will tell his friends that he considers himself amply repaid for all his work. We say these things now, that you may fully understand the necessity and importance of mastering this fundamental method of Yogi Breathing, instead of passing it by and trying some of the attractive looking variations given later on in this book. Again, we say to you: Start right, and right results will follow; but neglect your foundations and your entire building will topple over sooner or later.

Perhaps the better way to teach you how to develop the Yogi Complete Breath, would be to give you simple directions regarding the breath itself, and then follow up the same with general remarks concerning it, and then later on giving exercises for developing the chest, muscles and lungs which have been allowed to remain in an undeveloped condition by imperfect methods of breathing. Right here we wish to say that this Complete Breath is not a forced or abnormal thing, but on the contrary is a going back to first principles—a return to Nature. The healthy adult savage and the healthy infant of civilization both breathe in this manner, but civilized man has adopted unnatural methods of living, clothing, etc., and has lost his birthright. And we wish to remind the reader that the Complete Breath does not necessarily call for the complete filling of the lungs at every inhalation. One may inhale the average amount of air, using the Complete Breathing Method and distributing the air inhaled, be the quantity large or small, to all parts of the lungs. But one should inhale a series of full Complete Breaths several times a day, whenever opportunity offers, in order to keep the system in good order and condition.

The following simple exercise will give you a clear idea of what the Complete Breath is:

1. Stand or sit erect. Breathing through the nostrils, inhale steadily, first filling the lower part of the lungs, which is accomplished by bringing into play the diaphragm, which descending exerts a gentle pressure on the abdominal organs, pushing forward the front walls of the abdomen. Then fill the middle part of the lungs, pushing out the lower ribs, breast-bone and chest. Then fill the higher portion of the lungs, protruding the upper chest, thus lifting the chest, including the upper six or seven pairs of ribs. In the final movement, the lower part of the abdomen will be slightly drawn in, which movement gives the lungs a support and also helps to fill the highest part of the lungs.

   At first reading it may appear that this breath consists of three distinct movements. This, however, is not the correct idea. The inhalation is continuous, the entire chest cavity from the lowered diaphragm to the highest point of the chest in the region of the collar-bone, being expanded with a uniform movement. Avoid a jerky series of inhalations, and strive to attain a steady continuous action. Practice will soon overcome the tendency to divide the inhalation into three movements, and will result in a uniform continuous breath. You will be able to complete the inhalation in a couple of seconds after a little practice.
2. Retain the breath a few seconds.

3. Exhale quite slowly, holding the chest in a firm position, and having the abdomen in a little and lifting it upward slowly as the air leaves the lungs. When the air is entirely exhaled, relax the chest and abdomen. A little practice will render this part of the exercise easy, and the movement once acquired will be afterwards performed almost automatically.

It will be seen that by this method of breathing all parts of the respiratory apparatus is brought into action, and all parts of the lungs, including the most remote air cells, are exercised. The chest cavity is expanded in all directions. You will also notice that the Complete Breath is really a combination of Low, Mid and High Breaths, succeeding each other rapidly in the order given, in such a manner as to form one uniform, continuous, complete breath.

You will find it quite a help to you if you will practice this breath before a large mirror, placing the hands lightly over the abdomen so that you may feel the movements. At the end of the inhalation, it is well to occasionally slightly elevate the shoulders, thus raising the collarbone and allowing the air to pass freely into the small upper lobe of the right lung, which place is sometimes the breeding place of tuberculosis.

At the beginning of practice, you may have more or less trouble in acquiring the Complete Breath, but a little practice will make perfect, and when you have once acquired it you will never willingly return to the old methods.

Chapter 9

Physiological Effect of the Complete Breath

Scarcely too much can be said of the advantages attending the practice of the Complete Breath. And yet the student who has carefully read the foregoing pages should scarcely need to have pointed out to him such advantages.

The practice of the Complete Breath will make any man or woman immune to Consumption and other pulmonary troubles, and will do away with all liability to contract "colds," as well as bronchial and similar weaknesses. Consumption is due principally to lowered vitality attributable to an insufficient amount of air being inhaled. The impairment of vitality renders the system open to attacks from disease germs. Imperfect breathing allows a considerable part of the lungs to remain inactive, and such portions offer an inviting field for bacilli, which invading the weakened tissue soon produce havoc.

Good healthy lung tissue will resist the germs, and the only way to have good healthy lung tissue is to use the lungs properly.

Consumptives are nearly all narrow-chested. What does this mean? Simply that these people were addicted to improper habits of breathing, and consequently their chests failed to develop and expand. The man who practices the Complete Breath will have a full broad chest, end the narrow-chested man may develop his chest to normal proportions if he will but adopt this mode of breathing. Such people must develop their chest cavities if they value their lives. Colds may often be prevented by practicing a little vigorous Complete Breathing whenever you feel that you are being unduly exposed. When chilled, breathe vigorously a few minutes, and you will feel a glow all over your body. Most colds can be cured by Complete Breathing and partial fasting for a day.

The quality of the blood depends largely upon its proper oxygenation in the lungs, and if it is under-oxygenated it becomes poor in quality and laden with all sorts of impurities, and the system suffers from lack of nourishment, and often becomes actually poisoned by the waste products remaining uneliminated in the blood. As the entire body, every organ and every part, is dependent upon the blood for nourishment, impure blood must have a serious effect upon the entire system. The remedy is plain—practice the Yogi Complete Breath.

The stomach and other organs of nutrition suffer much from improper breathing. Not only are they ill nourished by reason of the lack of oxygen, but as the food must absorb oxygen from the blood and become oxygenated before it can be digested and assimilated, it is readily seen how digestion and assimilation is impaired by incorrect breathing. And when assimilation is not normal, the system receives less and less nourishment, the appetite fails, bodily vigor decreases, and energy diminishes, and the man withers and declines. All from the lack of proper breathing.

Even the nervous system suffers from improper breathing, inasmuch as the brain, the spinal cord, the nerve centers, and the nerves themselves, when improperly nourished by means of the blood, become poor and inefficient instruments for generating, storing and transmitting the nerve currents. And improperly nourished they will become if sufficient oxygen is not absorbed through the lungs. There is another aspect of the case whereby the nerve currents themselves, or rather the force from which the nerve currents spring, becomes lessened from want of proper breathing, but this belongs to another phase of the subject which is treated off in other chapters of this book, and our purpose here is to direct your attention to the fact that the mechanism of the nervous system is rendered inefficient as an instrument for conveying nerve force, as the indirect result of a lack of proper breathing.

The effect of the reproductive organs upon the general health is too well known to be discussed at length here, but we may be permitted to say that with the reproductive organs in a weakened condition the entire system feels the reflex action and suffers sympathetically. The Complete Breath produces a rhythm which is Nature's own plan for keeping this important part of the system in normal condition, and, from the first, it will be noticed that the reproductive functions are strengthened and vitalized, thus, by sympathetic reflex action, giving tone to the whole system. By this, we do not mean that the lower sex impulses will be aroused; far from it. The Yogis are advocates of continence and chastity, and have learned to control the animal passions. But sexual control does not mean sexual weakness, and the Yogi teachings are that the man or woman whose reproductive organism is normal and healthy, will have a stronger will with which to control himself or herself. The Yogi believes that much of the perversion of this wonderful part of the system comes from a lack of normal health, and results from a morbid rather than a normal condition of these organs. A little careful consideration of this question will prove that the Yogi teachings are right. This is not the place to discuss the subject fully, but the Yogis know that sex-energy may be conserved and used for the development of the body and mind of the individual, instead of being dissipated in unnatural excesses as is the wont of so many uninformed people. By special request we will give in this book one of the favorite Yogi exercises for this purpose. But whether or not the student wishes to adopt the Yogi theories of continence and clean-living, he or she will find that the Complete Breath will do more to restore health to this part of the system than anything else ever tried. Remember, now, we mean normal health, not undue development. The sensualist will find that normal means a lessening of desire rather than an increase; the weakened man or woman will find a toning up and a relief from the weakness which has heretofore depressed him or her. We do not wish to be misunderstood or misquoted on this subject. The Yogis' ideal is a body strong in all its parts, under the control of a masterful and developed Will, animated by high ideals.

In the practice of the Complete Breath, during inhalation, the diaphragm contracts and exerts a gentle pressure upon the liver, stomach and other organs, which in connection with the rhythm of the lungs acts as a gentle massage of these organs and stimulates their actions, and encourages normal functioning. Each inhalation aids in this internal exercise, and assists in causing a normal circulation to the organs of nutrition and elimination. In High or Mid Breathing the organs lose the benefit accruing from this internal massage.

The Western world is paying much attention to Physical Culture just now, which is a good thing. But in their enthusiasm they must not forget that the exercise of the external muscles is not everything. The internal organs also need exercise, and Nature's plan for this exercise is proper breathing. The diaphragm is Nature's principal instrument for this internal exercise. Its motion vibrates the important organs of nutrition and elimination, and massages and kneads them at each inhalation and exhalation, forcing blood into them, and then squeezing it out, and imparting a general tone to the organs. Any organ or part of the body which is not exercised gradually atrophies and refuses to function properly, and lack of the internal exercise afforded by the diaphragmatic action leads to diseased organs. The Complete Breath gives the proper motion to the diaphragm, as well as exercising the middle and upper chest. It is indeed "complete" in its action.

From the standpoint of Western physiology alone, without reference to the Oriental philosophies and science, this Yogi system of Complete Breathing is of vital importance to every man, woman and child who wishes to acquire health and keep it. It's very simplicity keeps thousands from seriously considering it, while they spend fortunes in seeking health through complicated and expensive "systems." Health knocks at their door and they answer not. Verily the stone which the builders reject is the real cornerstone of the Temple of Health.

Chapter 10

A Few Bits of Yogi Lore

We give below three forms of breath, quite popular among the Yogis. The first is the well-known Yogi Cleansing Breath, to which is attributed much of the great lung endurance found among the Yogis. They usually finish up a breathing exercise with this Cleansing Breath, and we have followed this plan in this book. We also give the Yogi Nerve Vitalizing Exercise, which has been handed down among them for ages, and which has never been improved on by Western teachers of Physical Culture, although some of them have "borrowed" it from teachers of Yoga. We also give the Yogi Vocal Breath, which accounts largely for the melodious, vibrant voices of the better class of the Oriental Yogis. We feel that if this book contained nothing more than these three exercises, it would be invaluable to the Western student. Take these exercises as a gift from your Eastern brothers and put them into practice.

The Yogi Cleansing Breath

The Yogis have a favorite form of breathing which they practice when they feel the necessity of ventilating and cleansing the lungs. They conclude many of their other breathing exercises with this breath, and we have followed this practice in this book. This Cleansing Breath ventilates and cleanses the lungs, stimulates the cells and gives a general tone to the respiratory organs, and is conducive to their general healthy condition. Besides this effect, it is found to greatly refresh the entire system. Speakers, singers, etc., will find this breath especially restful, after having tired the respiratory organs.

1. Inhale a complete breath.
2. Retain the air a few seconds.
3. Pucker up the lips as if for a whistle (but do not spell out the cheeks), then exhale a little air through the opening, with considerable vigor. Then stop for a moment, retaining the air, and then exhale a little more air. Repeat until the air is completely exhaled. Remember that considerable vigor is to be used in exhaling the air through the opening in the lips.

This breath will be found quite refreshing when one is tired and generally "used up." A trial will convince the student of its merits. This exercise should be practiced until it can be performed naturally and easily, as it is used to finish up a number of other exercises given in this book, and it should be thoroughly understood.

The Yogi Nerve Vitalizing Breath

This is an exercise well known to the Yogis, who consider it one of the strongest nerve stimulants and invigorants known to man. Its purpose is to stimulate the Nervous System, develop nerve force, energy and vitality. This exercise brings a stimulating pressure to bear on important nerve centers, which in turn stimulate and energize the entire nervous system, and send an increased flow of nerve force to all parts of the body.

1. Stand erect.
2. Inhale a Complete Breath, and retain same.
3. Extend the arms straight in front of you, letting them be somewhat limp and relaxed, with only sufficient nerve force to hold them out.
4. Slowly draw the hands back toward the shoulders, gradually contracting the muscles and putting force into them, so that when they reach the shoulders the fists will be so tightly clenched that a tremulous motion is felt.
5. Then, keeping the muscles tense, push the fists slowly out, and then draw them back rapidly (still tense) several times.
6. Exhale vigorously through the mouth.
7. Practice the Cleansing Breath.

The efficiency of this exercise depends greatly upon the speed of the drawing back of the fists, and the tension of the muscles, and, of course, upon the full lungs. This exercise must be tried to be appreciated. It is without equal as a "bracer," as our Western friends put it.

The Yogi Vocal Breath

The Yogis have a form of breathing to develop the voice. They are noted for their wonderful voices, which are strong, smooth and clear, and have a wonderful trumpet-like carrying power. They have practiced this particular form of breathing exercise which has resulted in rendering their voices soft, beautiful and flexible, imparting to it that indescribable, peculiar floating quality, combined with great power. The exercise given below will in time impart the above-mentioned qualities, or the Yogi Voice, to the student who practices it faithfully. It is to be understood, of course, that this form of breath is to be used only as an occasional exercise, and not as a regular form of breathing.

1. Inhale a Complete Breath very slowly, but steadily, through the nostrils, taking as much time as possible in the inhalation.
2. Retain for a few seconds.
3. Expel the air vigorously in one great breath, through the wide opened mouth.
4. Rest the lungs by the Cleansing Breath.

Without going deeply into the Yogi theories of sound-production in speaking and singing, we wish to say that experience has taught them that the timbre, quality and power of a voice depends not alone upon the vocal organs in the throat, but that the facial muscles, etc., have much to do with the matter. Some men with large chests produce but a poor tone, while others with comparatively small chests produce tones of amazing strength and quality. Here is an interesting experiment worth trying: Stand before a glass and pucker up your mouth and whistle, and note the shape of your mouth and the general expression of your face. Then sing or speak as you do naturally, and see the difference. Then start to whistle again for a few seconds, and then, *without changing the position of your lips or face*, sing a few notes and notice what a vibrant, resonant, clear and beautiful tone is produced.

Chapter 11

The Seven Yogi Developing Exercises

The following are the seven favorite exercises of the Yogis for developing the lungs, muscles, ligaments, air cells, etc. They are quite simple but marvelously effective. Do not let the simplicity of these exercises make you lose interest, for they are the result of careful experiments and practice on the part of the Yogis, and are the essence of numerous intricate and complicated exercises, the non-essential portions being eliminated and the essential features retained.

1. The Retained Breath

This is a very important exercise which tends to strengthen and develop the respiratory muscles as well as the lungs, and its frequent practice will also tend to expand the chest. The Yogis have found that an occasional holding of the breath, after the lungs have been filled with the Complete Breath, is very beneficial, not only to the respiratory organs but to the organs of nutrition, the nervous system and the blood itself. They have found that an occasional holding of the breath tends to purify the air which has remained in the lungs from former inhalations, and to more fully oxygenate the blood. They also know that the breath so retained gathers up all the waste matter, and when the breath is expelled it carries with it the effete matter of the system, and cleanses the lungs just as a purgative does the bowels. The Yogis recommend this exercise for various disorders of the stomach, liver and blood, and also find that it frequently relieves bad breath, which often arises from poorly ventilated lungs. We recommend students to pay considerable attention to this exercise, as it has great merits. The following directions will give you a clear idea of the exercise:

1. Stand erect.
2. Inhale a Complete Breath.
3. Retain the air as long as you can comfortably.
4. Exhale vigorously through the open mouth.
5. Practice the Cleansing Breath.

At first you will be able to retain the breath only a short time, but a little practice will also show a great improvement. Time yourself with a watch if you wish to note your progress.

2. Lung Cell Stimulation

This exercise is designed to stimulate the air cells in the lungs, but beginners must not overdo it, and in no case should it be indulged in too vigorously. Some may find a slight dizziness resulting from the first few trials, in which case let them walk around a little and discontinue the exercise for a while.

1. Stand erect, with hands at sides.
2. Breathe in very slowly and gradually.
3. While inhaling, gently tap the chest with the finger tips, constantly changing position.
4. When the lungs are filled, retain the breath and pat the chest with the palms of the hands.
5. Practice the Cleansing Breath.

This exercise is very bracing and stimulating to the whole body, and is a well-known Yogi practice. Many of the air cells of the lungs become inactive by reason of incomplete breathing, and often become almost atrophied. One who has practiced imperfect breathing for years will find it not so easy to stimulate all these ill-used air cells into activity all at once by the Complete Breath, but this exercise will do much toward bringing about the desired result, and is worth study and practice.

3. Rib Stretching

We have explained that the ribs are fastened by cartilages, which admit of considerable expansion. In proper breathing, the ribs play an important part, and it is well to occasionally give them a little special exercise in order to preserve their elasticity. Standing or sitting in unnatural positions, to which many of the Western people are addicted, is apt to render the ribs more or less stiff and inelastic, and this exercise will do much to overcome same.

1. Stand erect.
2. Place the hands one on each side of the body, as high up under the armpits as convenient, the thumbs reaching toward the back, the palms on the side of the chest and the fingers to the front over the breast.
3. Inhale a Complete Breath.
4. Retain the air for a short time.
5. Then gently squeeze the sides, at the same time slowly exhaling.
6. Practice the cleansing breath.

Use moderation in this exercise and do not overdo its

4. Chest Expansion

The chest is quite apt to be contracted from bending over one's work, etc. This exercise is very good for the purpose of restoring natural conditions and gaining chest expansion.

1. Stand erect.
2. Inhale a Complete Breath.
3. Retain the air.

4. Extend both arms forward and bring the two clenched fists together on a level with the shoulder.
5. Then swing back the fists vigorously until the arms stand out straight sideways from the shoulders.
6. Then bring back to Position 4, and swing to Position 5. Repeat several times.
7. Exhale vigorously through the opened mouth.
8. Practice the Cleansing Breath.

Use moderation and do not overdo this exercise.

5. Walking Exercise

1. Walk with head up, chin drawn slightly in, shoulders back, and with measured tread.
2. Inhale a Complete Breath, counting (mentally) 1, 2, 3, 4, 5, 6, 7, 8, one count to each step, making the inhalation extend over the eight counts.
3. Exhale slowly through the nostrils, counting as before—1, 2, 3, 4, 5, 6, 7, 8—one count to a step.
4. Rest between breaths, continuing walking and counting, I, 2, 3, 4, 5, 8, 7, 8, one count to a step.
5. Repeat until you begin to feel tired. Then rest for a while, and resume at pleasure. Repeat several times a day.

Some Yogis vary this exercise by retaining the breath during a 1, 2, 3, 4, count, and then exhale in an eight-step count. Practice whichever plan seems most agreeable to you.

6. Morning Exercise

1. Stand erect in a military attitude, head up, eyes front, shoulders back, knees stiff, hands at sides.
2. Raise body slowly on toes, inhaling a Complete Breath, steadily and slowly.
3. Retain the breath for a few seconds, maintaining the same position.
4. Slowly sink to first position, at the same time slowly exhaling the air through the nostrils.
5. Practice Cleansing Breath.
6. Repeat several times, varying by using right leg alone, then left leg alone.

7. Stimulating Circulation

1. Stand erect.
2. Inhale a Complete Breath and retain.
3. Bend forward slightly and grasp a stick or cane steadily and firmly, and gradually exerting your entire strength upon the grasp.
4. Relax the grasp, return to first position, and slowly exhale.
5. Repeat several times.
6. Finish with the Cleansing Breath.

This exercise may be performed without the use of a stick or cane, by grasping an imaginary cane, using the will to exert the pressure. The exercise is a favorite Yogi plan of stimulating the circulation by driving the arterial blood to the extremities, and drawing back the venous blood to the heart and lungs that it may take up the oxygen which has been inhaled with the air. In cases of poor circulation there is not enough blood in the lungs to absorb the increased amount of oxygen inhaled, and the system does not get the full benefit of the improved breathing.

In such cases, particularly, it is well to practice this exercise, occasionally with the regular Complete Breathing exercise.

Chapter 12

Seven Minor Yogi Exercises

This chapter is composed of seven minor Yogi Breathing Exercises, bearing no special names, but each distinct and separate from the others and having a different purpose in view. Each student will find several of these exercises best adapted to the special requirements of his particular case. Although we have styled these exercises "minor exercises," they are quite valuable and useful, or they would not appear in this book. They give one a condensed course in "Physical Culture" and "Lung Development," and might readily be "padded out" and elaborated into a small book on these subjects. They have, of course, an additional value, as Yogi Breathing forms a part of each exercise. Do not pass them by because they are marked "minor." Some one or more of these exercises may be just what you need. Try them and decide for yourself.

Exercise I

1. Stand erect with hands at sides.
2. Inhale Complete Breath.
3. Raise the arms slowly, keeping them rigid until the hands touch over head.
4. Retain the breath a few minutes with hands over head.
5. Lower hands slowly two sides, exhaling slowly at same time.
6. Practice Cleansing Breath.

Exercise II

1. Stand erect, with arms straight In front of you.
2. Inhale Complete Breath and retain.
3. Swing arms back as far as they will go; then back to first position; then repeat several times, returning the breath all the while.
4. Exhale vigorously through mouth.
5. Practice Cleansing Breath.

Exercise III

1. Stand erect with arms straight In front of you,
2. Inhale Complete Breath.
3. Swing arms around in a circle, backward, a few times. Then reverse a few times, retaining the breath all the while.

You may vary this by rotating them alternately like the sails of a windmill.

4. Exhale the breath vigorously through the mouth.
5. Practice Cleansing Breath.

Exercise IV

1. Lie on the floor with your face downward and palms of hands flat upon the floor by your sides.
2. Inhale Complete Breath and retain.
3. Stiffen the body and raise yourself up by the strength of your arms until you rest on your hands and toes
4. Then lower yourself to original position. Repeat several times.
5. Exhale vigorously through your mouth.
6. Practice Cleansing Breath.

Exercise V

1. Stand erect with your palms against the wall.
2. Inhale Complete Breath and retain.
3. Lower the chest to the wall, resting your weight on your hands.
4. Then raise yourself back with the arm muscles alone, keeping the body stiff.
5. Exhale vigorously through the mouth.
6. Practice Cleansing Breath.

Exercise VI

1. Stand erect with arms "akimbo," that is, with hands resting around the waist and elbows standing out.
2. Inhale Complete Breath and retain.
3. Keep legs and hips stiff and bend well forward, as If bowing, at the same time exhaling slowly.
4. Return to first position and take another Complete Breath.
5. Then bend backward, exhaling slowly.
6. Return to first position and take a Complete Breath.
7. Then bend sideways, exhaling slowly. (Vary by bending to right and then to left.)
8. Practice Cleansing Breath.

Exercise VII

1. Stand erect, or sit erect, with straight spinal column.
2. Inhale a Complete Breath, but instead of inhaling in a continuous steady stream, take a series of short, quick "sniffs," as if you were smelling aromatic salts or ammonia and did not wish to get too strong a "whiff." Do not exhale any of these little breaths, but add one to the other until the entire lung space Is filled.
3. Retain for a few seconds.
4. Exhale through the nostrils in a long, restful, sighing breath.
5. Practice Cleansing Breath.

Chapter 13

Vibration and Yogi Rhythmic Breathing

All is in vibration. From the tiniest atom to the greatest sun, everything is in a state of vibration. There is nothing in absolute rest in nature. A single atom deprived of vibration would wreck the universe. In incessant vibration the universal work is performed. Matter is being constantly played upon by energy and countless forms and numberless varieties result, and yet even the forms and varieties are not permanent. They begin to change the moment they are created, and from them are born innumerable forms, which in turn change and give rise to newer forms, and so on and on, in infinite succession. Nothing is permanent in the world of forms, and yet the great Reality is unchangeable. Forms are but appearances—they come, they go, but the Reality is eternal and unchangeable.

The atoms of the human body are in constant vibration. Unceasing changes are occurring. In a few months there is almost a complete change in the matter composing the body, and scarcely a single atom now composing your body will be found in It a few months hence. Vibration, constant vibration. Change, constant change.

In all vibration is to be found a certain rhythm. Rhythm pervades the universe. The swing of the planets around the sun; the rise and fall of the sea; the beating of the heart; the ebb and flow of the tide; all follow rhythmics laws. The rays of the sun reach us; the rain descends upon us, in obedience to the same law. All growth is but an exhibition of this law. All motion is a manifestation of the law of rhythm.

Our bodies are as much subject to rhythmic laws as is the planet in its revolution around the sun. Much of the esoteric side of the Yogi Science of Breath is based upon this known principle of nature. By falling in with the rhythm of the body, the Yogi manages to absorb a great amount of Prana, which he disposes of to bring about results desired by him. We will speak of this at greater length later on.

The body which you occupy is like a small inlet running in to the land from the sea. Although apparently subject only to its own laws, it is really subject to the ebb and flow of the tides of the ocean. The great sea of life is swelling and receding, rising and falling, and we are responding to its vibrations and rhythm. In a normal condition we receive the vibration and rhythm of the great ocean of life, and respond to it, but at times the mouth of the inlet seems choked up with debris, and we fail to receive the impulse from Mother Ocean, and in harmony manifests within us.

You have heard how a note on a violin, if sounded repeatedly and in rhythm, will start into motion vibrations which will in time destroy a bridge. The same result is true when a regiment of soldiers crosses a bridge, the order being always given to "break step" on such an occasion, lest the vibration bring down both bridge and regiment. These manifestations of the effect of rhythmic motion will give you an idea of the effect on the body of rhythmic breathing. The whole system catches the vibration and becomes in harmony with the will, which causes the rhythmic motion of the lungs, and while in such complete harmony will respond readily to orders from the will. With the body thus attuned, the Yogi finds no difficulty in increasing the circulation in any part of the body by an order from the will, and in the same way he can direct an increased current of nerve force to any part or organ, strengthening and stimulating it.

In the same way the Yogi by rhythmic breathing "catches the swing," as it were, and is able to absorb and control a greatly increased amount of prana, which is then at the disposal of his will. He can and does use it as a vehicle for sending forth thoughts to others and for attracting to him all those whose thoughts are keyed in the same vibration. The phenomena of telepathy, thought transference, mental healing, mesmerism, etc., which subjects are creating such an interest in the Western world at the present time, but which have been known to the Yogis for centuries, can be greatly increased and augmented If the person sending forth the thoughts will do so after rhythmic breathing. Rhythmic breathing will increase the value of mental healing, magnetic healing, etc., several hundred per cent.

In rhythmic breathing the main thing to be acquired is the mental idea of rhythm. To those who know anything of music, the idea of measured counting is familiar. To others, the rhythmic step of the soldier: "Left, right; left, right; left, right; one, two, three, four; one, two, three, four," will convey the idea.

The Yogi bases his rhythmic time upon a unit corresponding with the beat of his heart. The heart beat varies in different persons, but the heart beat unit of each person is the proper rhythmic standard for that particular individual in his rhythmic breathing. Ascertain your normal heart beat by placing your fingers over your pulse, and then count: "1, 2, 3, 4, 5, 6; 1, 2, 3, 4, 5, 6," etc., until the rhythm becomes firmly fixed in your mind. A little practice will fix the rhythm, so that you will be able to easily reproduce it. The beginner usually inhales in about six pulse units, but he will be able to greatly increase this by practice.

The Yogi rule for rhythmic breathing is that the units of inhalation and exhalation should be the same, while the units for retention and between breaths should be one-half the number of those of inhalation and exhalation.

The following exercise in Rhythmic Breathing should be thoroughly mastered, as it forms the basis of numerous other exercises, to which reference will be made later.

1. Sit erect, in an easy posture, being sure to hold the chest, neck and head as nearly in a straight line as possible, with shoulders slightly thrown back and hands resting easily on the lap. In this position the weight of the body is largely supported by the ribs and the position may be easily maintained. The Yogi has found that

one cannot get the best effect of rhythmic breathing with the chest drawn in and the abdomen protruding.

2. Inhale slowly a Complete Breath, counting six pulse units.
3. Retain, counting three pulse units.
4. Exhale slowly through the nostrils, counting six pulse units.
5. Count three pulse beats between breaths.
6. Repeat a number of times, but avoid fatiguing yourself at the start.
7. When you are ready to close the exercise, practice the cleansing breath, which will rest you and cleanse the lungs.

After a little practice you will be able to increase the duration of the inhalations and exhalations, until about fifteen pulse units are consumed. In this increase, remember that the units for retention and between breaths is one-half the units for inhalation and exhalation.

Do not overdo yourself in your effort to increase the duration of the breath, but pay as much attention as possible to acquiring the "rhythm," as that is more important than the length of the breath. Practice and try until you get the measured "swing" of the movement, and until you can almost "feel" the rhythm of the vibratory motion throughout your whole body. It will require a little practice and perseverance, but your pleasure at your improvement will make the task an easy one. The Yogi is a most patient and persevering man, and his great attainments are due largely to the possession of these qualities.

Chapter 14

Phenomena of Yogi Psychic Breathing

With the exception of the instructions in the Yogi Rhythmic Breathing, the majority of the exercises heretofore given in this book relate to the physical plane of effort, which, while highly important in itself, is also regarded by the Yogis as in the nature of affording a substantial basis for efforts on the psychic and spiritual plane. Do not, however, discard or think lightly of the physical phase of the subject, for remember that it needs a sound body to support a sound mind, and also that the body is the temple of the Ego, the lamp in which burns the light of the Spirit. Everything is good in its place, and everything has its place. The developed man is the "all-around man," who recognizes body, mind and spirit and renders to each its due. Neglect of either is a mistake which must be rectified sooner or later; a debt which must be repaid with interest.

We will now take up the Psychic phase of the Yogi Science of Breath in the shape of a series of exercises, each exercise carrying with it its explanation.

You will notice that in each exercise rhythmic breathing is accompanied with the instructions to "carry the thought" of certain desired results. This mental attitude gives the Will a cleared track upon which to exercise its force. We cannot, in this work, go into the subject of the power of the Will, and must assume that you have some knowledge of the subject. If you have no acquaintance with the subject, you will find that the actual practice of the exercises themselves will give you a much clearer knowledge than any amount of theoretical teaching, for as the old Hindu proverb says, "He who tastes a grain of mustard seed knows more of its flavor than he who sees an elephant load of it."

1. General Directions for Yogi Psychic Breathing

The basis of all Yogi Psychic Breathing is the Yogi Rhythmic Breath, instruction regarding which we gave in our last chapter. In the following exercises, in order to avoid useless repetition, we will say merely, "Breathe Rhythmically," and then give the instruction for the exercise of the psychic force, or directed Will power working in connection with the rhythmic breath vibrations. After a little practice you will find that you will not need to count after the first rhythmic breath, as the mind will grasp the idea of time and rhythm and you will be able to breathe rhythmically at pleasure, almost automatically. This will leave the mind clear for the sending of the psychic vibrations under the direction of the Will. (See the following first exercise for directions in using the Will.)

2. Prana Distributing

Lying flat on the floor or bed, completely relaxed, with hands resting lightly over the Solar Plexus (over the pit of the stomach, where the ribs begin to separate), breathe rhythmically. After the rhythm is fully established *will* that each inhalation will draw in an increased supply of prana or vital energy from the Universal supply, which will be taken up by the nervous system and stored in the Solar Plexus. At each exhalation will that the prana or vital energy is being distributed all over the body, to every organ and part; to every muscle, cell and atom; to nerve, artery and vein; from the top of your head to the soles of your feet; invigorating, strengthening and stimulating every nerve; recharging every nerve center; sending energy, force and strength all over the system. While exercising the will, try to form a mental picture of the inrushing prana, coming in through the lungs and being taken up at once by the Solar Plexus, then with the exhaling effort, being sent to all parts of the system, down to the finger tips and down to the toes. It is not necessary to use the Will with an effort. Simply commanding that which you wish to produce and then making the mental picture of it is all that is necessary. Calm command with the mental picture is far better than forcible willing, which only dissipates force needlessly. The above exercise is most helpful and greatly refreshes and strengthens the nervous system and produces a restful feeling all over the body.

It is especially beneficial In cases where one is tired or feels a lack of energy.

3. Inhibiting Pain

Lying down or sitting erect, breath rhythmically, holding the thought that you are inhaling prana. Then when you exhale, send the prana to the painful part to re-establish the circulation and nerve current. Then inhale more prana for the purpose of driving out the painful condition; then exhale, holding the thought that you are driving out the pain. Alternate the two above mental commands, and with one exhalation stimulate the part and with the next drive out the pain. Keep this up for seven breaths, then practice the Cleansing Breath and rest a while. Then try it again until relief comes, which will be before long. Many pains will be found to be relieved before the seven breaths are finished. If the hand is placed over the painful part, you may get quicker results. Send the current of prana down the arm and into the painful part.

4. Directing the Circulation

Lying down or sitting erect, breathe rhythmically, and with the exhalations direct the circulation to any part you wish, which may be suffering from imperfect circulation. This is effective in cases of cold feet or in cases of headache, the blood being sent downward in both cases, in the first case warming the feet, and in the latter, relieving the brain from too great pressure.

In the case of headache, try the Pain Inhibiting first, then follow with sending the blood downward. You will often feel a warm feeling in the legs as the circulation moves downward. The circulation is largely under the control of the will and rhythmic breathing renders the task easier.

5. Self-Healing

Lying in a relaxed condition, breathe rhythmically, and command that a good supply of prana be inhaled. With the exhalation, send the prana to the affected part for the purpose of stimulating it. Vary this occasionally by exhaling, with the mental command that the diseased condition be forced out and disappear. Use the hands in this exercise, passing them down the body from the head to the affected part. In using the hands in healing yourself or others always hold the mental image that the prana is flowing down the arm and through the finger tips into the body, thus reaching the affected part and healing it. Of course we can give only general directions in this book without taking up the several forms of disease in detail, but a little practice of the above exercise, varying it slightly to fit the conditions of the case, will produce wonderful results. Some Yogis follow the plan of placing both hands on the affected part, and then breathing rhythmically, holding the mental image that they are fairly pumping prana into the diseased organ and part, stimulating it and driving out diseased conditions, as pumping into a pail of dirty water will drive out the latter and fill the bucket with fresh water. This last plan is very effective if the mental image of the pump is clearly held, the inhalation representing the lifting of the pump handle and the exhalation the actual pumping.

6. Healing Others

We cannot take up the question of the psychic treatment of disease by prana in detail in this book, as such would be foreign to its purpose. But we can and will give you simple, plain instructions whereby you may be enabled to do much good in relieving others. The main principle to remember is that by rhythmic breathing and controlled thought you are enabled to absorb a considerable amount of prana, and are also able to pass it into the body of another person, stimulating weakened parts and organs and imparting health and driving out diseased conditions. You must first learn to form such a clear mental image of the desired condition that you will be able to actually feel the influx of prana, and the force running down your arms and out of your finger tips into the body of the patient. Breathe rhythmically a few times until the rhythm is fairly established, then place your bands upon the affected part of the body of the patient, letting them rest lightly over the part. Then follow the "pumping" process described to the preceding exercise (Self-Healing) and fill the patient full of prana until the diseased condition is driven out. Every once in a while raise the hands and "flick" the fingers as if you were throwing off the diseased condition. It is well to do this occasionally and also to wash the hands after treatment, as otherwise you may take on a trace of the diseased condition of the patient. Also practice the Cleansing Breath several times after the treatment. During the treatment let the prana pour into the patient in one continuous stream, allowing yourself to be merely the pumping machinery connecting the patient with the universal supply of prana, and allowing it to flow freely through you. You need not work the hands vigorously, but simply enough that the prana freely reaches the affected parts. The rhythmic breathing must be practiced frequently during the treatment, so as to keep the rhythm normal and to afford the prana a free passage. It is better to place the hands on the bare skin, but where this is not advisable or possible place them over the clothing. Vary above method occasionally during the treatment by stroking the body gently and softly with the finger tips, the fingers being kept slightly separated. This is very soothing to the patient. In cases of long standing you may find it helpful to give the mental command in words, such as "get out, get out," or "be strong, be strong," as the case may be, the words helping you to exercise the will more forcibly and to the point. Vary these instructions to suit the needs of the case, and use your own judgment and inventive faculty. We have given you the general principles and you can apply them in hundreds of different ways. The above apparently simple instruction, if carefully studied and applied, will enable one to accomplish all that the leading "magnetic healers" are able to, although their "systems" are more or less cumbersome and complicated. They are using prana ignorantly and calling it "magnetism." If they would combine rhythmic breathing with their "magnetic" treatment they would double their efficiency.

7. Distant Healing

Prana colored by the thought of the sender may be projected to persons at a distance, who are willing to receive it, and healing work done in this way. This is the secret of the "absent healing," of which the Western world has heard so much of late years. The thought of the healer sends forth and colors the prana of the sender, and it flashes across space and finds lodgment in the psychic mechanism of the patient. It is unseen, and like the Marconi waves, it passes through intervening obstacles and seeks the person attuned to receive it. In order to treat persons at a distance, you must form a mental image of them until you can feel yourself to be en rapport with them. This is a psychic process dependent upon the mental imagery of the healer. You can feel the sense of rapport when it is established, it manifesting in a sense of nearness. That is about as plain as we can describe it. It may be acquired by a little practice, and some will get it at the first trial. When rapport is established, say mentally to the distant patient, "I am sending you a supply of vital force or power, which will invigorate you and heal you." Then picture the prana as leaving your mind with each exhalation of rhythmic breath, and traveling across space instantaneously and reaching the patient and healing him. It is not necessary to fix certain hours for treatment, although you may do so if you wish. The receptive condition of the patient, as he is expecting and opening himself up to your psychic force, attunes him to receive your vibrations whenever you may send them. If you agree upon hours, let him place himself in a relaxed attitude and receptive condition.

The above is the great underlying principle of the "absent treatment" of the Western world. You may do these things as well as the most noted healers, with a little practice.

Chapter 15

More Phenomena of Yogi Psychic Breathing

1. Thought Projection

Thoughts may be projected by following the last mentioned method (Distant Healing) and others will feel the effect of thought so sent forth, it being remembered always that no evil thought can ever injure another person whose thoughts are good. Good thoughts are always positive to bad ones, and bad ones always negative to good ones. One can, however, excite the interest and attention of another by sending him thought waves in this way, charging the prana with the message he wishes to convey. If you desire another's love and sympathy, and possess love and sympathy for him, you can send him thoughts of this kind with effect, providing your motives are pure. Never, however, attempt to influence another to his hurt, or from impure or selfish motives, as such thoughts only recoil upon the sender with redoubled force, and injure him, while the innocent party is not affected. Psychic force when legitimately used is all right, but beware of "black magic" or improper and unholy uses of it, as such attempts are like playing with a dynamo, and the person attempting such things will be surely punished by the result of the act itself. However, no person of impure motives ever acquires a great degree of psychic power, and a pure heart and mind is an invulnerable shield against improper psychic power. Keep yourself pure and nothing can hurt you.

2. Forming an Aura

If you are ever in the company of persons of a low order of mind, and you feel the depressing influence of their thought, breathe rhythmically a few times, thus generating an additional supply of prana, and then by means of the mental image method surround yourself with an egg-shaped thought aura, which will protect you from the gross thought and disturbing influences of others.

3. Recharging Yourself

If you feel that your vital energy is at a low ebb, and that you need to store up a new supply quickly, the best plan is to place the feet close together (side by side, of course) and to lock the fingers of both hands in any way that seems the most comfortable.

This closes the circuit, as it were, and prevents any escape of prana through the extremities. Then breathe rhythmically a few times, and you will feel the effect of the recharging.

4. Recharging Others

If some friend is deficient in vitality you may aid him by sitting in front of him, your toes touching his, and his hands in yours. Then both breathe rhythmically, you forming the mental image of sending prana into his system, and he holding the mental image of receiving the prana. Persons of weak vitality or passive will should be careful with whom they try this experiment, as the prana of a person of evil desires will be colored with the thoughts of that person, and may give him a temporary influence over the weaker person. The latter, however, may easily remove such influence by closing the circuit (as before mentioned) and breathing a few rhythmic breaths, closing with the Cleansing Breath.

5. Charging Water

Water may be charged with prana, by breathing rhythmically, and holding the glass of water by the bottom, in the left hand, and then gathering the fingers of the right hand together and shaking them gently over the water, as if you were shaking drops of water off of your finger tips into the glass. The mental image of the prana being passed into the water must also be held. Water thus charged is found stimulating to weak or sick persons, particularly if a healing thought accompanies the mental image of the transfer of the prana. The caution given in the last exercise applies also to this one, although the danger exists only in a greatly lessened degree.

6. Acquiring Mental Qualities

Not only can the body be controlled by the mind under direction of the will, but the mind itself can be trained and cultivated by the exercise of the controlling will. This, which the Western world knows as "Mental Science," etc., has proved to the West portions of that truth which the Yogi has known for ages. The mere calm demand of the Will accomplish wonders in this direction, but if the mental exercise is accompanied by rhythmic breathing, the effect is greatly increased. Desirable qualities may be acquired by holding the proper mental image of what is desired during rhythmic breathing. Poise and Self Control, desirable qualities; increased power, etc., may be acquired in this way. Undesirable qualities may be eliminated by cultivating the opposite qualities. Any or all the "Mental Science" exercises, "treatments" and "affirmations" may be used with the Yogi Rhythmic Breath. The following is a good general exercise for the acquirement and development of desirable mental qualities:

Lie in a passive attitude, or sit erect. Picture to yourself the qualities you desire to cultivate, seeing yourself as possessed of the qualities, and demanding that your mind develop the quality. Breathe rhythmically, holding the mental picture firmly. Carry the mental picture with you as much as possible, and endeavor to live up to the ideal you have set up in your mind.

You will find yourself gradually growing up to your ideal. The rhythm of the breathing assists the mind in forming new combinations, and the student who has followed the Western system will find the Yogi Rhythmic a wonderful ally in his "Mental Science" works.

7. Acquiring Physical Qualities

Physical qualities may be acquired by the same methods as above mentioned in connection with mental qualities. We do not mean, of course, that short men can be made tall, or that amputated limbs may be replaced, or similar miracles. But the expression of the countenance may be changed; courage and general physical characteristics improved by the control of the Will, accompanied by rhythmic breathing. As a man thinks so does he look, act, walk, sit, etc. Improved thinking will mean improved looks and actions. To develop any part of the body, direct the attention to it, while breathing rhythmically, holding the mental picture that you are sending an increased amount of prana, or nerve force, to the part, and thus increasing its vitality and developing it. This plan applies equally well to any part of the body which you wish to develop. Many Western athletes use a modification of this plan in their exercises. The student who has followed our instructions so far will readily understand how to apply the Yogi principles in the above work. The general rule of exercise is the same as in the preceding exercise (acquiring Mental Qualities). We have touched upon the subject of the cure of physical ailments in preceding pages.

8. Controlling the Emotions

The undesirable emotions, such as Fear, Worry, Anxiety, Hate, Anger, Jealousy, Envy, Melancholy, Excitement, Grief, etc., are amenable to the control of the Will, and the Will is enabled to operate more easily in such cases if rhythmic breathing is practiced while the student is "willing." The following exercise has been found most effective by the Yogi students, although the advanced Yogi has but little need of it, as he has long since gotten rid of these undesirable mental qualities by growing spiritually beyond them. The Yogi student, however, finds the exercise a great help to him while he is growing.

Breathe rhythmically, concentrating the attention upon the Solar Plexus, and sending to it the mental command "Get Out." Send the mental command firmly, just as you begin to exhale, and form the mental picture of the undesirable emotions being carried away with the exhaled breath. Repeat seven times, and finish with the Cleansing Breath, and then see how good you feel. The mental command must be given "in earnest," as trifling will not do the work.

9. Transmutation of the Reproductive Energy

The Yogis possess great knowledge regarding the use and abuse of the reproductive principle in both sexes. Some hints of this esoteric knowledge have filtered out and have been used by Western writers on the subject, and much good has been accomplished in this way. In this little book we cannot do more than touch upon the subject, and omitting all except a bare mention of theory, we will give a practical breathing exercise whereby the student will be enabled to transmute the reproductive energy into vitality for the entire system, instead of dissipating and wasting it in lustful indulgences in or out of the marriage relations. The reproductive energy is creative energy, and may be taken up by the system and transmuted into strength and vitality, thus serving the purpose of regeneration instead of generation. If the young men of the Western world understood these underlying principles they would be saved much misery and unhappiness in after years, and would be stronger mentally, morally and physically.

This transmutation of the reproductive energy gives great vitality to those practicing it. They will be filled with great vital force, which will radiate from them and will manifest in what has been called "personal magnetism." The energy thus transmuted may be turned into new channels and used to great advantage. Nature has condensed one of its most powerful manifestations of prana into reproductive energy, as its purpose is to create. The greatest amount of vital force is concentrated in the smallest area. The reproductive organism is the most powerful storage battery in animal life, and its force can be drawn upward and used, as well as expended in the ordinary functions of reproduction, or wasted in riotous lust. The majority of our students know something of the theories of regeneration; and we can do little more than to state the above facts, without attempting to prove them.

The Yogi exercise for transmuting reproductive energy is simple. It is coupled with rhythmic breathing, and can be easily performed. It may be practiced at any time, but is specially recommended when one feels the instinct most strongly, at which time the reproductive energy is manifesting and may be most easily transmuted for regenerative purposes. The exercise is as follows: Keep the mind fixed on the idea of Energy, and away from ordinary sexual thoughts or imaginings. If these thoughts come into the mind do not be discouraged, but regard them as manifestations of a force which you intend using for the purposes of strengthening the body and mind. Lie passively or sit erect, and fix your mind on the idea of drawing the reproductive energy upward to the Solar Plexus, where it will be transmuted and stored away as a reserve force of vital energy. Then breathe rhythmically, forming the mental image of drawing up the reproductive energy with each inhalation. With each inhalation make a command of the Will that the energy be drawn upward from the reproductive organization to the Solar Plexus. If the rhythm is fairly established and the mental image is clear, you will be conscious of the upward passage of the energy, and will feel its stimulating effect. If you desire an increase in mental force, you may draw it up to the brain instead of to the Solar Plexus, by giving the mental command and holding the mental image of the transmission to the brain. The man or woman doing metal creative work, or bodily creative work, will be able to use this creative energy in their work by following the above exercise, drawing up the energy with the inhalation and sending it forth with the exhalation. In this last form of exercise, only such portions as are needed in the work will pass into the work being done, the balance remaining stored up in the Solar Plexus. You will understand, of course, that it is not the reproductive fluids which are drawn up and used, but the etheripranic energy which animates the latter, the soul of the reproductive organism, as it were. It is usual to allow the head to bend forward easily and naturally during the transmuting exercise.

10. Brain Stimulating

The Yogis have found the following exercise most useful in stimulating the action of the brain for the purpose of producing clear thinking and reasoning. It has a wonderful effect in clearing the brain and nervous system, and those engaged in mental work will find it most useful to them, both in the direction of enabling them to do better work and also as a means of refreshing the mind and clearing it after arduous mental labor.

Sit in an erect posture, keeping the spinal column straight, and the eyes well to the front, letting the hands rest on the upper part of the legs. Breathe rhythmically, but instead of breathing through both nostrils as in the ordinary exercises, press the left nostril close with the thumb, and inhale through the right nostril. Then remove the thumb, and close the right nostril with the finger, and then exhale through the left nostril. Then, without changing the fingers, inhale through the left nostril, and changing fingers, exhale through the right. Then inhale through right and exhale through left, and so on, alternating nostrils as above mentioned, closing the unused nostril with the thumb or forefinger. This is one of the oldest forms of Yogi breathing, and is quite important and valuable, and is well worth of acquirement. But it is quite amusing to the Yogis to know that to the Western world this method is often held out as being the "whole secret" of Yogi Breathing. To the minds of many Western readers, "Yogi Breathing" suggests nothing more than a picture of a Hindu, sitting erect, and alternating nostrils in the act of breathing. "Only this and nothing more." We trust that this little work will open the eyes of the Western world to the great possibilities of Yogi Breathing, and the numerous methods whereby it may be employed.

11. The Grand Yogi Psychic Breath

The Yogis have a favorite form of psychic breathing which they practice occasionally, to which has been given a Sanskrit term of which the above is a general equivalent. We have given it last, as it requires practice on the part of the student in the line of rhythmic breathing and mental imagery, which he has now acquired by means of the preceding exercises. The general principles of the Grand Breath may be summed up in the old Hindu saying: "Blessed is the Yogi who can breathe through his bones." This exercise will fill the entire system with prana, and the student will emerge from it with every bone, muscle, nerve, cell, tissue, organ and part energized and attuned by the prana and the rhythm of the breath. It is a general house-cleaning of the system, and he who practices it carefully will feel as if he had been given a new body, freshly created, from the crown of his head to the tips of his toes. We will let the exercise speak for itself.

1. Lie in a relaxed position, at perfect ease.
2. Breathe rhythmically until the rhythm is perfectly established.

3. Then, inhaling and exhaling, form the mental image of the breath being drawn up through the bones of the legs, and then forced out through them; then through the bones of the arms; then through the top of the skull; then through the stomach; then through the reproductive region; then as if it were traveling upward and downward along the spinal column; and then as if the breath were being inhaled and exhaled through every pore of the skin, the whole body being filled with prana and life.
4. Then (breathing rhythmically) send the current of prana to the Seven Vital Centers, in turn, as follows, using the mental picture as in previous exercises:
   a) To the forehead.
   b) To the back of the head.
   c) To the base of the brain.
   d) To the Solar Plexus.
   e) To the Sacral Region (lower part of the spine).
   f) To the region of the navel.
   g) To the reproductive region.

   Finish by sweeping the current of prana, to and fro from head to feet several times.
5. Finish with Cleansing Breath.

Chapter 16

Yogi Spiritual Breathing

The Yogis not only bring about desired mental qualities and properties by will-power coupled with rhythmic breathing, but they also develop spiritual faculties, or rather aid in their unfoldment, in the same way. The Oriental philosophies teach that man has many faculties which are at present in a dormant state, but which will become unfolded as the race progresses. They also teach that man, by the proper effort of the will, aided by favorable conditions, may aid in the unfoldment of these spiritual faculties, and develop them much sooner than in the ordinary process of evolution. In other words, one may even now develop spiritual powers of consciousness which will not become the common property of the race until after long ages of gradual development under the law of evolution. In all of the exercises directed toward this end, rhythmic breathing plays an important part. There is of course no mystic property in the breath itself which produces such wonderful results, but the rhythm produced by the Yogi breath is such as to bring the whole system, including the brain, under perfect control, and in perfect harmony, and by this means, the most perfect condition is obtained for the unfoldment of these latent faculties.

In this work we cannot go deeply into the philosophy of the East regarding spiritual development, because this subject would require volumes to cover it, and then again the subject is too abstruse to interest the average reader. There are also other reasons, well known to occultists, why this knowledge should not be spread broadcast at this time. Rest assured, dear student, that when the time comes for you to take the next step, the way will be opened out before you. "When the chela (student) is ready, the guru (master) appears." In this chapter we will give you directions for the development of two phases of spiritual consciousness, i.e., (1) the consciousness of the identity of the Soul, and (2) the consciousness of the connection of the Soul with the Universal Life. Both of the exercises given below are simple, and consist of mental images firmly held, accompanied with rhythmic breathing. The student must not expect too much at the start, but must make haste slowly, and be content to develop as does the flower, from seed to blossom.

Soul Consciousness

The real Self is not the body or even the mind of man. These things are but a part of his personality, the lesser self. The real Self is the Ego, whose manifestation is in individuality. The real Self is independent of the body, which it inhabits, and is even independent of the mechanism of the mind, which it uses as an instrument. The real Self is a drop from the Divine Ocean, and is eternal and indestructible. It cannot die or be annihilated, and no matter what becomes of the body, the real Self still exists. It is the Soul. Do not think of your Soul as a thing apart from you, for YOU are the Soul, and the body is the unreal and transitory part of you which is changing in material every day, and which you will someday discard. You may develop the faculties so that they will be conscious of the reality of the Soul, and its independence of the body. The Yogi plan for such development is by meditation upon the real Self or Soul, accompanied by rhythmic breathing. The following exercise is the simplest form.

Exercise.—Place your body in a relaxed, reclining position. Breathe rhythmically, and meditate upon the real Self, thinking of yourself as an entity independent of the body, although inhabiting it and being able to leave it at will. Think of yourself, not as the body, but as a spirit, and of your body as but a shell, useful and comfortable, but not a part of the real You. Think of yourself as an independent being, using the body only as a convenience. While meditating, ignore the body entirely, and you will find that you will often become almost entirely unconscious of it, and will seem to be out of the body to which you may return when you are through with the exercise.

This is the gist of the Yogi meditative breathing methods, and if persisted in will give one a wonderful sense of the reality of the Soul, and will make him seem almost independent of the body. The sense of immortality will often come with this increased consciousness, and the person will begin to show signs of spiritual development which will be noticeable to himself and others. But he must not allow himself to live too much in the upper regions, or to despise his body, for he is here on this plane for a purpose, and he must not neglect his opportunity to gain the experiences necessary to round him out, nor must he fail to respect his body, which is the Temple of the Spirit.

The Universal Consciousness

The Spirit in man, which is the highest manifestation of his Soul, is a drop in the ocean of Spirit, apparently separate and distinct, but yet really in touch with the ocean itself, and with every other drop in it. As man unfolds in spiritual consciousness he becomes more and more aware of his relation to the Universal Spirit, or Universal Mind as some term it. He feels at times as if he were almost at-one-ment with it, and then again he loses the sense of contact and relationship. The Yogis seek to attain this state of Universal Consciousness by meditation and rhythmic breathing, and many have thus attained the highest degree of spiritual attainment possible to man in this stage of his existence. The student of this work will not need the higher instruction regarding adeptship at this time, as he has much to do and accomplish before he reaches that stage, but it may be well to initiate him into the elementary stages of the Yogi exercises for developing Universal Consciousness, and if he is in earnest he will discover means and methods whereby he may progress. The way is always opened to him who is ready to tread the path. The following exercise will be found to do much toward developing the Universal Consciousness in those who faithfully practice it.

Exercise.—Place your body in a reclining, relaxed position. Breathe rhythmically, and meditate upon your relationship with the Universal Mind of which you are but an atom. Think of yourself as being in touch with All, and at-onement with All. See All as One, and your Soul as a part of that One. Feel that you are receiving the vibrations from the great Universal Mind, and are partaking of its power and strength and wisdom. The two following lines of meditation may be followed.

(a) With each inhalation, think of yourself as drawing in to yourself the strength and power of the Universal Mind. When exhaling think of yourself as passing out to others that same power, at the same time being filled with love for every living thing, and desiring that it be a partaker of the same blessings which you are now receiving. Let the Universal Power circulate through you.

(b) Place your mind in a reverential state, and meditate upon the grandeur of the Universal Mind, and open yourself to the inflow of the Divine Wisdom, which will fill you with illuminating wisdom, and then let the same flow out from you to your brothers and sisters whom you love and would help.

This exercise leaves with those who have practiced it a new-found sense of strength, power and wisdom, and a feeling of spiritual exaltation and bliss. It must be practiced only in a serious, reverential mood, and must not be approached triflingly or lightly.

General Directions

The exercises given in this chapter require the proper mental attitude and conditions, and the trifler and person of a non-serious nature, or one without a sense of spirituality and reverence, had better pass them by, as no results will be obtained by such persons, and besides it is a wilful trifling with things of a high order, which course never benefits those who pursue it. These exercises are for the few who can understand them, and the others will feel no attraction to try them.

During meditation let the mind dwell upon the ideas given in the exercise, until it becomes clear to the mind, and gradually manifests in real consciousness within you. The mind will gradually become passive and at rest, and the mental image will manifest clearly. Do not indulge in these exercises too often, and do not allow the blissful state produced to render you dissatisfied with the affairs of everyday life, as the latter are useful and necessary for you, and you must never shirk a lesson, however disagreeable to you it may be. Let the joy arising from the unfolding consciousness buoy you up and nerve you for the trials of life, and not make you dissatisfied and disgusted. All is good, and everything has its place. Many of the students who practice these exercises will in time wish to know more. Rest assured that when the time comes we will see that you do not seek in vain. Go on in courage and confidence, keeping your face toward the East, from whence comes the rising Sun.

Peace be unto you, and unto all men.

AUM

PAPERBACK NON-FICTION

- 12 Years A Slave by Solomon Northup, ISBN: 9789390492374
- 51 Must Know Facts About Albert Einstein by GP Editors, ISBN: 9789354991486
- 51 Must Know Facts About Brain by GP Editors, ISBN: 9789354994371
- A Theory of Human Motivation by Abraham H. Maslow, ISBN: 9789354993732
- Becoming a Writer by Dorothea Brande, ISBN: 9789389157093
- Believe in Yourself by Joseph Murphy, ISBN: 9789388118385
- Chanakya Neeti by Chanakya, ISBN: 9789389716276
- Children's Objective Quiz by Azeem Ahmad Khan, ISBN: 9788180320781
- Creative Mind and Success by Ernest Holmes, ISBN: 9789354994661
- Delighting in God by AW Tozer, ISBN: 9788194748632
- Feeling is the Secret by Neville Goddard, ISBN: 9789389157109
- Five Chimneys by Olga Lengyel, ISBN: 9789354991127
- Five Lessons by Neville Goddard, ISBN: 9789354991134
- Gravity by George Gamow, ISBN: 9789388118484
- Great Speeches of Abraham Lincoln, ISBN: 9789380914336
- How to Attract Money by Joseph Murphy, ISBN: 9789388118408
- How to Develop Self Confidence and... by Dale Carnegie, ISBN: 9789387669000
- How to Enjoy Your Life and Your Job by Dale Carnegie, ISBN: 9789387669017
- How to Own Your Own Mind by Napoleon Hill, ISBN: 9789354991189
- How to Stop Worrying and Start Living by Dale Carnegie, ISBN: 9789380914817
- How to Use the Power of Prayer by Joseph Murphy, ISBN: 9789354994395
- How to Win Friends and Influence People by Dale Carnegie, ISBN: 9788180320217
- If You Want to Write by Brenda Ueland, ISBN: 9789389716290
- Know Your Worth by NK Sondhi, ISBN: 9788180320231
- Life in Corona by NK Sondhi, ISBN: 9789354990571

Develop your reading habit | **Gift books to your friends**

PAPERBACK NON-FICTION

- Madhubala by Manju Gupta, ISBN: 9789380914961
- Mahatma Gandhi by Romain Rolland, ISBN: 9789354994456
- Meditation and Its Methods by Swami Vivekananda, ISBN: 9789389716320
- Meditations by Marcus Aurelius, ISBN: 9789388118736
- Mein Kampf by Adolf Hitler, ISBN: 9789380914855
- Memory by William Walker Atkinson, ISBN: 9789390492800
- My Inventions: An Autobiography by Nikola Tesla, ISBN: 9789388118132
- Quiz For All by Azeem Ahmad Khan, ISBN: 9788180320897
- State and Revolution by Vladimir Ilich Lenin, ISBN: 9789354990922
- Stolen Legacy by George J.M. James, ISBN: 9789354994494
- Success Through a Positi. Mental Attitude by Napoleon Hill, ISBN: 9789390492435
- Tao Te Ching by Lao Tzu, ISBN: 9788194764823
- The Alchemy of Happiness by Al-Ghazzali, ISBN: 9789387669505
- The Art of Living by Epictetus, ISBN: 9789354993817
- The Art of Public Speaking by Dale Carnegie, ISBN: 9788180320422
- The Autobiography of a Yogi by Paramahansa Yogananda, ISBN: 9789380914602
- The Complete Prophecies of Nostradamus by Nostradamus, ISBN: 9789354994234
- The Dhammapada by Gautama Buddha, ISBN: 9789390492817
- The Dynamic Laws of Prosperity by Catherine Ponder, ISBN: 9789388118156
- The Elements of Style by William Strunk, ISBN: 9789389157123
- The Federalist Papers by Alexander Hamilton, ISBN: 9789390492862
- The Interpretation of Dreams by Sigmund Freud, ISBN: 9789390492879
- The Knowledge of the Holy by AW Tozer, ISBN: 9789389157130
- The Kybalion: Philo. of Egypt & Greece by Three Initiates, ISBN: 9789354994579
- The Magic of Faith by Joseph Murphy, ISBN: 9789388118743

Develop your reading habit | **Gift books to your friends**

PAPERBACK NON-FICTION

- The Miracles of Your Mind by Joseph Murphy, ISBN: 9788180320743
- The Path of Prosperity by James Allen, ISBN: 9789387669512
- The Power of Concentration by Theron Q. Dumont, ISBN: 9789388118064
- The Power of the Spoken Word by Florence Scovel Shinn, ISBN: 9789390492893
- The Problem of Increasing Human Energy by Nikola Tesla, ISBN: 9789354990953
- The Problems of Philosophy by Bertrand Russell, ISBN: 9789354994296
- The Quick and Easy Way to Effec. Speaking by Dale Carnegie, ISBN: 9789387669031
- The Science of Being Great by Wallace D. Wattles, ISBN: 9789354993886
- The Science of Getting Rich by Wallace D. Wattles, ISBN: 9788180320972
- The Science of Mind by Ernest Holmes, ISBN: 9789354993909
- The Secret of Imagining by Neville Goddard, ISBN: 9789354991271
- The Secret Teachings of All Ages by Manly P. Hall, ISBN: 9789390492046
- The Seven Laws of Teaching by John Milton Gregory, ISBN: 9789387669413
- The Story of My Life by Helen Keller, ISBN: 9789380914541
- The Success System that Never Fails by W.C. Stone, ISBN: 9789390492114
- The Ultimate Guide To Success by Julia Seton, ISBN: 9789390492350
- The Wit and Wisdom of Gandhi by Mahatma Gandhi, ISBN: 9789380914039
- The Yoga Sutras of Patanjali by Patanjali, ISBN: 9789389716351
- Think and Grow Rich by Napoleon Hill, ISBN: 9788180320255
- Thought Vibration by William Walker Atkinson, ISBN: 9789389157154
- Thoughts are Things by Prentice Mulford, ISBN: 9789354994326
- Up From Slavery by Booker T. Washington, ISBN: 9789380914565
- Value, Price, and Profit by Karl Marx, ISBN: 9789354993978
- Wake Up and Live by Dorothea Brande, ISBN: 9789387669574
- Who were the Shudras by Dr. B.R. Ambedkar, ISBN: 9789354991028

Develop your reading habit | **Gift books to your friends**